Dedicated to:

My father and mother, Ed and Marianne; my brothers and sisters, Ed, Ken, Patty, Janet, and Matt; and my two children, Justin and Carissa, for all of the life lessons we learned together.

Barbie in Real Life

Barbie Durham

© 2021 Barbie Durham

All rights reserved. No part of this publication may be reproduced, stored in a retrieval system, or transmitted in any form or by any means, electronic, mechanical, photocopying, recording, or otherwise without the prior permission of the author or in accordance with the provisions of the Copyright, Designs, and Patents Act 1988, or under the terms of any licence permitting limited copying issued by the Copyright Licensing Angency.

Published by:
The Ghost Publishing, USA

Paperback ISBN-13: 978-1-7371531-3-9
Ebook ISBN-13: 978-1-7371531-4-6

Printed in USA

Contents

Introduction xv

Chapter 1
It's Not a Life Sentence 1

    God's Assignments 1

    Will the Real Director Please Stand Up? 2

    Strengthen the New Narrative 3

    What Are You Going to Do About it? 3

Chapter 2
A Little About Me 5

    The Power in a Name 5

    There Were Six of Us 6

    The Love of Extended Family 7

    Moving to Arizona 9

Chapter 3
It's About to Change 11

    The Accent Had to Go 11

  The Real Reason We Moved 12

  Society Shifts 14

  I Found Him 15

Chapter 4
You're Going to Need Me 17

  The Unexpected Messenger 17

  So Many Changes 19

  The Apartment 19

  Father to the Fatherless 21

Chapter 5
The Promise to Mom 23

  Mom, too? 23

  Look After the Orphans 24

  The Promise Tested 26

Chapter 6
The Promise Fulfilled 29

  The Angel Revealed It All 29

  Unbelievable Reunion 30

Chapter 7
Healing the Father Wound 33

  The Wound Was Deep 33

  Let's Try Something Else 34

  Honor Him Anyway 37

Chapter 8
Creating My Own Family 39

Up in the Air and Everything 39

The Surprise of My Life 40

I'm Leaving 42

Chapter 9
Broken Beyond Repair 45

How Do I Come Back from That? 45

When God Hides You in Chaos 46

Chapter 10
Facts or Faith? 49

Prayerful Beginning 49

Intuition of a Mother 51

What Do You See? 53

Chapter 11
Wading in the Waiting 57

Aggressive Treatment 57

Praise Your Way Through It 58

What's Happening? 59

Just Tell Me 59

The Second Breath 60

The NFL Player 61

A Gift from a Stranger 62

The Last Second of the Game 65

Chapter 12
It's Time to Heal 69

He's Still Lying 69

Wrestling with God 72

The Ram Will Be There 74

Moving Forward 76

Pray for Him 77

Chapter 13
Guided by Dreams 81

The Powerful Subconscious 81

Bus Dream 82

Rescued from the Ocean Dream 82

Lost Purse Dream 83

Offensive Coach Dream 84

Chapter 14
The Solution 87

Acknowledgments 91

About the Author 93

Introduction

I love to inspire people to passionately pursue God.

I was a cheerleader in college, and I loved it. It was inspiring to me to lead people up onto their feet and enthusiastically watch them participate at these sporting events.

I have seen many amazing plays in the last second of a game that turned into unexpected outcomes, leaving both spectators and team players in awe.

Guess what? God has amazing plays in the game of life!

Your life is no different from a sporting event. No matter what is happening, or which direction it looks like a situation is going, when you walk with God, the game can always be won in the last three seconds.

- He is the master of the pivot move.
- The master of the comeback.
- The master of the turnaround.

There are plays that you will read in this book that happened in the last second of our game that miraculously changed the outcome.

Do you believe that God calls the plays in your life?

If you live your life 100% with that belief, then even when life throws unjust calls at you with penalties against your innocence, you will be able to withstand and trust the greatest coach you've ever played for.

It is in those heart-crushing times, when your clock is running out and your faith is severely tested, that you are given new legs to stand on.

Jesus tells us in John 14:12: "Very truly I tell you, whoever believes in me will do the works I have been doing, and they will do even greater things than these, because I am going to the Father."

When is His Church going to outlandishly believe Him for the miraculous signs and wonders of the sick being healed, the dead raised, and the oppressed delivered?

I believe the answer to that question is *now*!

It is time to get up on our feet and enthusiastically throw our prayers out into the deep and ask for the impossible in faith, trusting the divine outcome of our situations to Jesus.

I have a passion to believe that marriages will be completely restored. This institution, which represents a pure covenant made before God, has been ransacked by the societal effects of pornography, adultery, abuse, and abandonment.

Do you believe that God can restore this type of brokenness in your life even after the damage that has been done?

I absolutely do!

It is not going to happen until we look within ourselves first and deal with areas of unforgiveness, shame, and blame. When we return wholeheartedly to the holiness and purity of our marriage vows, God can step in for a miraculous comeback.

It is time to get back to the guidelines of marriage the way God arranged them.

He is the original creator of the institution and knows that marriage works best when one man and one woman commit to love each other for life. It is time to return to God with a repentant heart that makes us weep and a humble spirit toward our spouse for failing to be obedient in this area.

"Husbands, love your wives and do not be harsh with them" (Col. 3:19).

When we see the altars of our churches filled with people in this posture, we will be experiencing the revival that the Church has desperately needed.

Jesus says in Revelation 12:11 that we overcome by His blood and by the word of our testimony. Your testimony is a major component of your faith, and a much-needed asset to inspire others to believe God for their own miracles.

People are watching you, whether you know it or not. Your life itself is a walking testimony. Do you remember the story of Lazarus in John 11? Mary and Martha had asked Jesus to come to pray for their brother, who was ill. Jesus lingered, and because of that, Lazarus died.

Why didn't He come before all their pain?

In this journey to restoration, Jesus identified with their emotional suffering and wept with them. In verse 40, He says, "Did I not say to you that if you would believe you would see the glory of God?"

After four days of death, coupled with its stench, Jesus called Lazarus out of his tomb. From that day on, Lazarus was a walking testimony of Jesus as healer and many came to see him (John 12:9).

I speak life over your marriage, no matter the stench, and simply say to both of you as Jesus said, "If you believe you will see the glory of God."

I have a burning passion to remind men that they are men of valor, equipped by God to love. Their masculine energy is a gift to our world. When godly men realize that the command to love is given to them by God, they will step up to the plate, remembering that God will fully equip them in whatever area they lack. This kind of love that God gives them, the love to serve their wives, is not a feeling or an emotion, but an actual gift given to them by Him, and if used properly, will also strengthen society.

I pray for a fire-fueling movement that men will not only love and lead their families well, but that they will step into the arena of society and lend their strength to orphans, widows, and prisoners.

My hope is that when you are done reading this book, you will no longer question the moves God allows in your life. You will have a firm faith to withstand any assault and a new strength to believe God for miraculous interventions and divine turnarounds.

You will no longer be focused on what is wrong, but will look upward to the One who makes all things new. I hope this crushes the limiting beliefs that keep you stuck and sows a seed of courage into your heart.

Revival is on the horizon, and the greatest move of God we have ever seen is upon the Church.

The question is, will you throw your faith out there and call your Lazarus out of the tomb?

I am on my feet, cheering for the long-awaited arrival of our bridegroom, the Lord Jesus Christ.

Acts 2:17 says, "In the last days, I will pour out my Spirit on all people. Your sons and daughters will prophesy, your young men will see visions, your old men will dream dreams."

"He will turn the hearts of the parents to their children, and the hearts of the children to their parents" (Mal. 4:6).

Will you believe with me for greater things than we have yet seen?

Chapter 1
It's Not a Life Sentence

God's Assignments

We all come into this world naked and needing care from other human beings to survive. In a perfect world, each of us should have received nurturing love, safety, and security from our earliest memories.

But, here's the truth: this is not a perfect world.

Some of us did not receive that nurturing from early on. Some of us were raised in difficult, abusive environments. No doubt, ignorant stressed-out parents caused a lot of trouble in our lives.

Do you know what it feels like to be hurt by someone who said that they loved you? Whether it was emotional or physical abuse, the bleeding from your heart was profuse and the damage lingered for years. Experts say that time heals all wounds. Time passes, but it doesn't necessarily heal. The bruises may fade on the outside, but we carry the emotional scars with us for life.

There is an expiration date on blaming our parents for steering us in the wrong direction. Once we are old enough to take the wheel, the responsibility to heal lies with us.

After all, it was God, in His infinite wisdom, who assigned us to our families at birth.

God doesn't make mistakes. He uses our experiences, both good and bad, to mold us into an instrument that He can use for His purpose. That is, if we let Him. Our early experiences definitely shape us. Hard things happen to all of us. Yes, they hurt. Yes, we need time to heal from them, But, ultimately, if we don't deal with those early experiences, we can make decisions in our adult lives that keep the same narrative playing.

The challenge is finding the strength to climb up on top of our emotions and get a hold of the command center which is in our brains. This is the place to go to overturn the narrative. We can train our minds to rethink those experiences using a different lens: the lens of God.

We can all have a beautiful, stable adulthood, no matter what our early childhood looked like. When we walk with God, He changes the narrative for us.

Will the Real Director Please Stand Up?
Have you ever seen The Truman Show? It's a 1998 movie starring Jim Carrey. The set is a 24-hour, round-the-clock filming of one man's life. Everybody on the set knows it's just a movie, but the star does not know that his life is being filmed minute-by-minute by the master plan of a director behind a camera.

Just like that movie, God is the director of our lives. He is the master behind the camera, calling the scenes. He knew right where we were at the age of five, and He knows right where we are today.

Each season of our lives is a beautiful hand-crafted tapestry planned by the director, but sometimes it takes time to see it. He already knew every scene that would play out in your life: past, present, and future.

There is great joy in remembering past roles where happiness exploded onto the set of your heart and a deep longing was fulfilled. You were elated when life surprised you with a spouse, a baby, a house, or a job. There are tremendous moments in life that encapsulate the joy of being alive and experiencing the reward of love and longings met, but how are we to respond when scenes of life don't bring joy, but rather unimaginable pain and trauma?

We question how a loving director could have even written that into our script, let alone grapple with why.

Just like The Truman Show, our lives are being filmed in real time. There are no acting classes, no extra takes, and no rehearsals. We simply play out the scenes handed to us by the director.

I have begged God to retake several scenes in my life and film it again, but this time with a different ending; one where the victim is vindicated and the oppressor is held responsible, justice is served, nobody dies, the marriage is restored, and everyone lives happily ever after.

I long for happy endings, and I believe that the impossible is possible, just by adding a little bit of fight and fortitude.

Throughout the chapters of this book, you will find that it didn't always go that way in my life. Tears would flow like a broken cistern as the Director said, "I'm not rewriting this. This is my plan for your life."

There were many scenes where I felt like I'd hit a brick wall going 1,200 mph. The lights to the set would get turned off, the cameramen would go home, and I would be left in the dark sprawled out on the floor unable to move, unable to speak, and barely able to breathe.

Pain like this creates a dark, scary place in your mind to be ultimately avoided.

We try to control our world, but the truth is, we are not in control. The less we resist the reality of that, the sooner we get through the lesson. There is something to be gained in every hardship. There is something being added to your character and the scope of your vision when you are broken and humbled by what life has handed you.

Strengthen the New Narrative
Someone close to you will inevitably let you down. Being let down is part of life. Letdowns can be mere moments of disappointments done by others that are forgivable. We are all flawed human beings in a process of becoming better versions of ourselves. Forgiveness should be our middle names. It should be the baton of grace we quickly extend to anyone who is truly repentant of the pain they caused us.

That is the beauty of loving another human being.

But, what do we do when the pendulum swings to the other side and a life-altering offense results in damage to your soul and body, leaving your spirit on life support just to keep breathing?

Is it possible to recover from these types of assaults?

Yes, it is, but it will not be a journey for the weak at heart. You are not in that category. Once you start educating yourself and realize that all your pointing fingers need to be aimed at your own heart, the beauty of rewriting your story begins. You are strong, and you have the ability within to create a new narrative.

Is it possible that we are the ones resisting what God is trying to accomplish inside of us? A great place to start rewriting the narrative is to change the questions you're asking yourself. Instead of asking "why" something happened to you or "why" God allowed it to happen, try asking, "what" purpose did God have in mind for me to learn from it?

Maybe the offense happened in your family of origin. Maybe it happened in the family you built. It doesn't matter. It happened.

What Are You Going to Do About it?
We've established that some type of pain has come into your life and it has deeply affected your heart and well-being. Now the question is, "What are you going to do about it?"

The miracle stories you will read in this book are the truth. They are mingled together with the mess, the pain, and the hand of God's deliverance. They happened, and each one built a catalyst for me to continue to believe the Director no matter how hard life got, and it got hard.

Barbie in Real Life is the realistic version of societal issues women face in our culture. There are definitive concerns unique to our culture that have ripped at the moral compass and hearts of women everywhere.

The feminine experience has been tainted by the effects of pornography, abuse, betrayal, and abandonment. The idyllic assumptions of the '60s, which were supposed to include much happiness for Barbie, have been replaced with messages from church counsel to endure, to suffer for Jesus under the guise of misusing the term submission in the face of abuse.

God has something to say to His women: He sees you, and He hears you—and so do I.

It is God's heart for us to live whole lives; "Beloved, I pray that you may prosper in all things and be in health, even as your soul prospers" (3 John 1:2). I choose the latter. I choose for my soul to prosper, and I want to help you do the same.

Contained in this book, you will find the hope and faith to unlock things within yourself that are holding you hostage to pain. You will find your voice again. You will find the freedom to make tough decisions. This is your time to live a life with complete emotional healing and freedom. You have one life, and I would like to help you to live it to the fullest. As you walk through the pages of this book, I will be with you in spirit, and believe me when I say, "I am praying for you." This book was written with you in my heart.

Chapter 2
A Little About Me

The Power in a Name

Few people know that for the first day of my newborn life, my name was Janet, not Barbie.

While driving down the road in the family station wagon, my father had an epiphany. The song *Barbara Ann* was blaring on the radio as his toe tapped to the beat. He knew at that moment that when he returned to the hospital to take me home, he would do whatever it took to change my name from Janet Eileen, to the popular name at that time, Barbara Ann.

Chorus:
A Ba-Ba-Ba-Ba-Barbara Ann
Ba-Ba-Ba-Ba-Barbara Ann
Barbara Ann
Take my hand
Barbara Ann
You got me rockin' and a rollin'
Rockin' and a reelin'
Barbara Ann
Ba-Ba-Ba-Barbara Ann

He was so determined that he spent an extra two hours demanding that the staff change the birth certificate. "Sir, we can't do that. It has never been done before," came the response from the nurses. Guess what? It happened that day! My father refused to take me home until they did it.

The tune is definitely catchy, and first became popular when a group called The Regents first recorded it in 1958. It became number 13 on the Billboard Hot 100 chart when they released it in 1961. By 1965, it reached record-breaking popularity when The Beach Boys recorded their version of it. The number one movie of 1960 was Swiss Family Robinson, and the number one song that year was Theme From a Summer Rose, by Percy Faith.

But one epiphany wasn't enough for my father; he had another one. It resonated in his mind that I should also be named Barbie because of the popularity of the first Barbie doll. That doll was born in March of 1959 by Ruth Handler. She actually named the doll Barbie after her own daughter, Barbara Ann, which Barbie was a popular nickname for.

Ruth's philosophy behind creating the doll was that, through this doll, every little girl would be allowed to become anything she wanted to be.

Barbie would always represent to every woman that she had choices.

It seemed that these attributes my father fought for attached themselves to me at birth and would give me strength to face the years that lay ahead of me.

- The Power of Music in the Soul
- The Fight to Make the Impossible Happen

My father had no way of knowing that, years later, Mattel would also introduce another doll: Barbie's boyfriend, Ken. Ken would be named after Ruth Handler's other child, her son—and Barbie's real brother—Ken.

Guess what? I already had an older brother named Ken. This platform was given to me at birth, and my brother and I were forever known as Barbie and Ken. I couldn't have made this stuff up if I tried.

There Were Six of Us
I grew up in a large family of six children. I was number four, somewhere lost in the middle of the tribe. A popular book by Dr. Kevin Leman titled, *The Birth Order Book*, with the subtitle, *Why You Are the Way You Are*, describes well the power of birth position in the family unit and how our personalities develop because of that rank. The book correctly identified my core nature as a middle child. I was definitely the peacemaker of the bunch.

We also mimicked a popular TV show, *The Brady Bunch*, with three boys and three girls.

Out of the six children, I turned out to be the only recessive gene in a sea of brown-eyed, brunette siblings. With my blonde hair and green eyes, I stood out like a lone albino seal in a zoo habitat.

I thought I was adopted. I'd overhear my parents explaining my physical differences to people who asked, saying that I belonged to the milkman. At four years old, I was very gullible; I didn't know that it was a cliché, and back then we really did have a milkman who delivered our milk to the house. I often wondered why he left me there.

We grew up on Long Island, New York, all of us talking with strong and noticeable New York accents. In this culture, you tend to interrupt each other often when speaking just to get a word in edgewise. To survive, everyone had to fight to have their voice heard and add their two cents. That was not always easy for the shy introverted child I was.

My mother was the oldest of seven children. We had a huge extended family that gathered together on most Sundays, usually at my grandparents' house. The memories in my heart are warm as I remember everyone trying to squeeze around tables to eat. There was always lots of laughter.

My father drove a city bus in Long Island Park for a living. He looked very handsome in his uniform. There were many days as a child when I walked with my Mom to the bus stop near our home to board his bus and do the last two hours of his route with him in the afternoon. I adored my father, and I loved being with him.

He was very kind to his passengers, and they seemed to engage with him easily. I sat right behind him and watched gleefully as he entertained his passengers with jokes. He was personable and took the time to get to know each one of them.

I loved seeing my Dad happy and strong, and I was proud of him.

I remember when he taught me to ride my bike without training wheels. It took a while for me to get the hang of balancing without falling off. One day, it clicked. I started pedaling. The only problem was, I began pedaling right into a four-way-stop intersection. I could hear my dad running behind me yelling, "Stop!"

I was crying. "Daddy, I don't know how to stop!"

Right before I pedaled into that intersection my dad caught my bike by the edge of the seat and stopped me. I had never been happier to have my dad close by.

Fathers play such an important role in the family.

My mother was a gracious hostess. When someone would stop by to visit, she'd always put on a pot of coffee, even if they said they didn't want any. That wasn't an option in our home. She'd say, "Don't be silly; sit down, you'll have a cup of coffee!"

She was a stay-at-home mom and cooked and cleaned like no one's business. She loved each one of us and did her best to care for her family.

The Love of Extended Family

At eight years old, my parents sent me to live with an aunt and uncle for a year. They sent my two sisters to live together with another aunt and uncle. Our parents said that they needed to work out some things and that they would come and get us when they were done.

I was young and never questioned why. I just believed them and trusted them. I had no idea what they were working out, but when you read the "why" in the next chapter, if will make the hair on your arms stand up.

All of a sudden, the dynamics of family as I had come to know it, abruptly changed. I was no longer the fourth middle child lost in the bunch. In my aunt and uncle's home, I was the baby of three children. I received the love, affection, and attention every child deserves while growing up.

I loved my aunt and uncle. He was a detective, and my aunt had this amazing laugh that I can still hear to this day. Every time she laughed, I laughed right along with her. Don't you just love people like that? They both had big hearts which they lavishly shared with me.

Every night, my uncle purposely laid his gun on the dining room table in full view—a place where everyone could see it. On my second day there, while my uncle was upstairs sleeping from having worked the night shift, I picked it up to look at it. My aunt walked in to find me with the gun in my hand and gently told me to put it down—carefully.

That night, my uncle scooped me up into his lap and showed me his gun. He asked me if I had any questions. He very lovingly told me to never touch his gun again when it was on the table. That talk ended with laughter and hugs.

You know what? I never touched his gun again. Looking back, I know that God was teaching my young heart what real discipline looks like.

My mother and father occasionally came to visit. I didn't cry for them or beg to go home. I had two cousins who were both older than me and I would run off and play with them. It felt like any other day.

I didn't realize until many years later that when the time came for me to go back home, my aunt and uncle had wanted to keep me. It broke their hearts to send me back. They saw me thriving, but they knew I needed to be with my brothers and sisters and my parents. So, home I went.

My parents had bought a new house during the time I had been away. We moved from Long Island to Hempstead to a red and white home with a basement. My father did a great job maintaining the landscaping, and most weekends I would be out there helping him.

One day I had stayed home from school because I wasn't feeling well. I went outside to help my father who was building a garden in the front yard. It was a hot day. After a few hours, he took off his shirt. So, you know what I did? I took mine off, too! I was eight years old. He laughed hysterically and said, "If your mother were here, she wouldn't like that. You need to put your shirt back on."

At the time, I didn't understand why. I mean, I was hot, too.

The attachment I had to my father was enormous. Any chance I had, I wanted to be with him and mimic everything he did.

Moving to Arizona
Four years later, my father decided to pack up the family and move us 2,450 miles west to Phoenix. He said it was because he had allergies.

I remember the day we left New York. My father had put my mother (who was now pregnant with our youngest brother), my two sisters, and me on a Greyhound bus to travel the 2,450-miles to Arizona. He and my brothers drove the U-Haul carrying the furniture.

My sister Patty and I made up a game to pass the time. We dared each other to do some absurd thing down the aisle to the bathroom in the back. It didn't count unless you did it both ways and returned to your seat. She dared me to skip on one leg, touching each seat as I passed by. As I turned to go back, she was watching and laughing hysterically.

Patty and I had a seemingly uncanny ability to just look at each other and giggle uncontrollably, like most young girls. I don't recall the other passengers laughing at us, though. I guess we weren't as funny as we thought. When I got back to my seat, we melted into a puddle of tears from laughing at ourselves.

We finally arrived in Arizona. We fully expected to see teepees and Indians living in them like we'd read in our New York textbooks. When we stepped off the bus, we were surprised to see that Phoenix looked just like a normal city and not the desert wilderness habitat we had imagined.

I had no idea that in one year my life would soon change so rapidly that I wouldn't even be the same person I started out as.

I would face crisis upon crisis, but I would also make the best decision I would ever make in my life.

Chapter 3

It's About to Change

The Accent Had to Go

Can you think of anything more painful to a seventh-grader than to start a new school mid-year? It can feel like a suicide mission to parade yourself in front of a new class and find your seat.

I made my grand entrance with a knot in my stomach as their glares checked me out, up one side and down the other. All their social cliques and groups had already been formed. Where would I fit in?

Every story has a silver lining if you look for it and mine was no different. My sister Patty was right by my side.

Even though she was two years older than me, we ended up starting school together and in the same class. That began in kindergarten when my parents decided I should start school at four years old. I wanted to believe that they did it because they saw the genius in me. But who am I kidding? They had six kids. Keeping me occupied was a solid solution to maintaining their sanity.

Through all twelve years of my education, I lived the illusion of being a twin with my sister. I enjoyed every minute of it. Teachers often would get Patty and I confused as to who was who, even though Patty was a brunette and I was a blonde.

Together, we arrived on planet Arizona with matching dueling New York accents that confused all the students. We found out quickly that the other kids didn't understand a lot of our words.

That had to change. I was quite determined to alter words like dog, water, and coffee as those words really accentuated my accent.

Many New Yorkers have a strange habit of adding "er" to words even though they're not there. For instance, if your name is Linda, we will call you "Linder" for the rest of your life.

I remember one day bringing home some school friends and my well-meaning father said, "You kids want some pizzer?"

I about died! Yes, that's the way you pronounce pizza in New York, you add the "er" to the end. Don't ask me why; there's no reasonable explanation. My friends asked, "What's pizzer?"

I quickly corrected my father, "Dad, it's pronounced pizza!"

I set this stage of my social drama to remind you how awkward it is to be twelve years old just trying to survive the normal transition from childhood to teenager.

Buckle up, I'm about to add more!

The Real Reason We Moved
I walked into the kitchen after school one day and came face to face with the real reason we moved to Arizona.

I swung open the front door, ran to the kitchen to get a snack, and much to my surprise there was a strange lady at the table.

When I got closer, I was stunned!

It was my father!

He was dressed like a woman from head to toe. He had on a wig, makeup including lipstick, a skirt, a blouse, pantyhose, and even ladies' shoes sitting with his legs crossed just like a woman.

Halloween was six months away. "Why in the world was he dressed like that?" I thought. I started to laugh, convinced he was just playing a trick. But when he told me to call him Aunt Sandra without cracking a smile, I knew he was dead serious.

I was beyond shaken. What. Was. Happening?

This was the plan my father had concocted to reveal to his family that he was a transvestite.

Many mental health experts used to think that this behavior had a sexual pleasure component attached to it. In contrast, most agree that there are simply individuals who enjoy the euphoria of getting in touch with the opposite-gendered side of themselves.

I had never heard of such a thing, nor did I know when it started for him.

Admittedly, in 1972, this was completely unacceptable, shameful, and not a topic discussed in society. No bureaus were counting the number of those struggling with gender identity, so there were no known percentages of the population to actually see how many were affected.

For a year, Aunt Sandra made appearances few and far between. His/Her secret brought much confusion. One minute, he was dressed like a man and I could call him Dad, and the next he was dressed like a woman and I had to call him Sandra.

Undoubtedly, there began to grow a new restlessness inside of him. This dichotomy resulted in an inner rage that spilled out against his children.

My father began to beat me. This loving man who I adored almost broke my arm on one occasion, and tossed me like a rag doll down the hallway on another.

Plain and simple, the presence of his children reminded him of his masculinity, something he was trying desperately to deny.

It became obvious that cross-dressing was not satisfying the root problem inside of him. He asked my mother to live happily with him as sisters instead of as husband and wife. Can you imagine? She made the very difficult decision to divorce him.

By the end of that seventh-grade year, he had abandoned our family to begin the treacherous journey of medically altering his body.

A year later, near my thirteenth birthday, my father showed up at our door to show us what he had done.

He had undergone gender reassignment surgery. The only thing that resembled the man I knew as my father was his six-foot stature. But now, he was a six-foot-tall lanky woman.

Gone were his prominent Adam's apple and his strong masculine features. The stubble on his face was replaced with smooth skin covered precisely with foundation and blush. I stumbled over calling him Karen, as he said his name was now.

He came inside to visit and I returned to my job of cleaning the bathroom. The next thing I knew, he came into the bathroom and started to fill the tub with water.

I tried not to look alarmed, but he began to undress. I wanted desperately to leave, but he told me to stay. He must have figured that, as we were all girls now, it was fine.

I didn't turn to look, but the bathroom was small and the mirror was large. His nudity danced before my eyes like a peacock among sparrows.

There was no denying the decapitation. The proof was in the pudding. He was completely female in all the right places.

I didn't say anything to him as I high-tailed it out of there as fast as I could. I buried my head in my pillow that night and wept tears of shame mixed with love, staining my cheeks with a poisonous concoction that I felt compelled to hide.

I missed my father.

My life had been turned upside-down as a result of his decision.

Because my mother chose to divorce him, he refused to provide alimony or help her financially. We were forced to move from our middle-class home into an apartment where I never felt safe.

Being that my mother didn't drive, she found a job where she could walk to work. The only shift she could find began at 3:15 pm and went to midnight. That gave me fifteen minutes with my mother after school for instructions on how to care for my baby brother (who was twelve months old) and what to cook for dinner.

I was thrown into adult responsibilities beyond my years.

I was angry, and I carried that underneath the surface of my teenage pride like a box of broken glass.

How do you grieve the loss of someone who is still alive, but not the person you once knew?

I wasn't doing a very good job of it. I grieved for my father every minute of every day.

When people would ask me, "What happened to him?"

I told them he died. To me, that was the truth. He died on that operating table.

Society Shifts
Forty-five years after the shame of my father's gender identity issue came out, society has swung the pendulum so far in the opposite direction that we now embrace and applaud gender identity and reassignment, even in our children.

One highly-publicized and socially-accepted transgender story is that of Bruce Jenner. He is best known for being an Olympic gold-medal-winning decathlete in the 1970s, and the stepfather of the Kardashian siblings on the reality show, *Keeping Up with the Kardashians*.

Bruce Jenner transitioned into a woman in 2017. He was a symbol of American masculinity. Today, he has become quite outspoken about being transgender and becoming Caitlyn Jenner. The world applauded his coming out and documented each step.

ESPN even presented him with the Arthur Ashe Award of Courage. This award is given to deserving athletes who overcome tremendous setbacks and health challenges. He was chosen over many other quite deserving athletes.

Walt Heyer, another former transsexual, had reconstruction surgery in 1983. He went by the name Laura for eight years before he says God helped him to be free of his identity issues.

He has quite a story. He actually switched his gender back to being male after a relationship with Jesus changed him forever.

He is the founder of the website, sexchangeregret.com, and the author of several books, including *Trading My Sorrows*, and *Paper Genders*.

Today, he is married to a woman and is enjoying the gender God originally created him to be. He shares his story freely to help others who are dealing with gender identity issues.

I Found Him
The longing for my father grew intense, and I could stand the pain no longer, so I set out to find him like an undercover private investigator.

After a full year of research, I found out where he lived—right by my orthodontist. Without telling a soul, I rode my bike there with my heart pounding so hard that it felt like it was coming out of my chest.

I saw his car pull up into the parking lot complex and I watched him from afar as he walked into his apartment. I took some deep breaths, got brave, and found the nerve to knock on his door. He answered, "May I help you? Are you selling girl scout cookies?"

I was shocked! He didn't recognize me. I said, "Dad, it's me, Barbie."

He invited me in, but his body was shaking. I had caught him off-guard. I stayed only for a few minutes because he was very uncomfortable.

He moved three days later and I never saw my father again.

At the age of fourteen, I was not only abandoned by him, but now I felt rejected. I stuffed that pain far into my heart and was determined to never speak of him again.

The story of my father wouldn't end there as I wanted it to, because God loved me too much and would reach for that pain years later to bring healing. It's a healing so remarkable that I've shared an entire chapter on it.

Chapter 4

You're Going to Need Me

The Unexpected Messenger

Who doesn't love receiving a gift from a loved one? But what if a stranger handed you a gift, with no strings attached, and that gift changed the course of your life? Now, that's a gift!

As a girl, I was obsessed with gymnastics. I carried the Olympic dream in my heart. Any spare time I had, you would find me practicing my flips in the front yard. This day was just like the rest, but in mid-cartwheel, I noticed new neighbors pulling up in their U-Haul.

I was twelve years old and we had only been in Arizona a few months. My father and his secret were alive and undisclosed right inside the walls of our home.

The first thing I thought of when I saw that truck was, do they have any kids my age? The doors flew open and out jumped five kids. To my surprise, the oldest was a girl my exact age. She immediately came over to introduce herself. "Hi, my name is Ricki," she said. Within five minutes she told me she had something to tell me.

As confidently as she could, she looked me straight in the eye and said, "God told us to choose this house over three others because He wanted us to give a message to our new neighbors."

Stunned, I asked, "What's the message?"

She replied, "God loves you!"

I had never heard that before.

My first response was, "You're twelve; God speaks to you?"

I grew up in a time where an old English proverb was prevalent: children are seen and not heard. Meaning, children were allowed to be present during a conversation, but were not allowed to speak unless spoken to first. Translated in my mind, that meant that adults were more important than children. With that ingrained in my mind, I figured that God was busy running the universe and didn't even see me.

Every week, I went to confession at our Catholic church because my parents took me there. I was taught to confess all of my sins to be right with God. The sins of a child are fairly limited, but I did beg God to forgive me for staining the carpet with my tomato juice because I'd received a severe beating from my father for that accident.

The message I held in my heart about God was, at best, that He was:

- ready to beat me over the head with a bat at the slightest mistake
- not very tolerant of my failure

That day, I learned that the real heart of God was first and foremost a message of love. His love found me in my secret pain, in my front yard, while the trauma of abuse was ravaging my soul.

The purity of Ricki's message, so blatant and simplistic, caught me off-guard. The fact that it came out of the heart of another child sparked my interest.

Ricki and I became instant friends and I marveled at her God stories. Her faith was real, and she knew God in a way that I didn't.

I remember one particular story she shared. She said her family had run out of money and could not buy any food. Her single mom and her siblings held hands together in their living room and asked God for help. Within the hour, someone randomly knocked on the door with bags of food.

My jaw dropped open. "Wow!"

She made the presence of God tangible and His Love something to be embraced every day of the week, not just on Sundays.

She invited me to go to church with her. I remember the day her pastor, Brother Butterfield, gave an invitation for anyone who wanted to receive Jesus into their heart to come down to the altar.

I stepped out and made my way to the front of the church and knelt down at the altar with this gentle pastor as he had me repeat this prayer, "Jesus, thank You for dying on the cross for my sins. I open the door of my life and receive You as my Savior and Lord. Thank You for forgiving my sins and giving me eternal life. Take control of the throne of my life."

From that moment, I became aware of the presence of God with me. It would take me years to overcome my misconceptions about God as it related to my failure and measuring up to His expectations, but that decision marked a turning point in my life and I began a love relationship with God that I never knew I could have, all because one person was bold enough to tell me that God loved me. It had nothing to do with religion or going to church. The best part was knowing that I had access to the Creator of the universe, through prayer, twenty-four hours a day, seven days a week.

If you don't know Jesus as your Lord and Savior, I would like to tell you what Ricki told me: God loves you. If you have never heard that before, it's true, and His heart is *for* you, not against you. Feel free to use the prayer that I prayed above to ask Jesus to be the Lord and Savior of your life right now. You will never regret it.

Unbeknownst to me, tragedy loomed in my very near future. I marvel at the timing Jesus had in bringing me His hope before these events happened. I would cling to Him in the bitter days ahead.

So Many Changes
Within a month, the first tragedy struck our home. My oldest brother Eddie was hit by a car. He was delivering newspapers for his paper route when a car hit him in a crosswalk. He only suffered a broken leg, but it was a major event in our home.

My other brother Ken took over his paper route. Unbelievably, Ken was also struck by a car in the same exact crosswalk one week later. His injuries were more serious. He was knocked off of his bicycle and lay unconscious on the blistering Arizona summer pavement. He received major burns to his back as well as broken bones and lacerations, but he too, survived.

If that wasn't enough, one month after that, the biggest crisis was the announcement of my father leaving our family to surgically alter his gender.

Before I could catch my breath, my brothers lay in bed in casts, my parents divorced, my father left us, and I had to say goodbye to my best friend Ricki, all the while, the moving van was packed with everything I knew in my life and heartlessly drove away.

The Apartment
Relocating takes time to acclimate to new surroundings. I was barely able to adjust to the first move from New York, but now adding another move so soon caused inner turmoil and meant the dread of starting another new school.

My father was kind enough to help us move into the new apartment. When we arrived with the first load, we noticed the management had not cleaned it. Because time was of the essence, I volunteered to stay behind and clean while the rest of my family made the one-hour trip back across town for a second load.

It was 4:00 pm when they left, but I fully expected them to be back before it got dark. Four o'clock turned into six o'clock, and my stomach started to rumble from hunger. It was starting to get dark outside. I reached for a light switch and found that the electricity had not yet been turned on. Soon, it was pitch black. I started to get scared.

Then the neighbors started arguing. They sounded like they were right outside the back door. When I realized that the lock on that door was broken and they could come in, I began to cry.

I noticed that the only light that I had was the light of the moon shining through the kitchen window. I moved the cooler my father had left me close to the window and knelt down. As the neighbors screamed, I sobbed deep tears of anguish and fear. This was the first time I would activate my faith.

I pretended the moon was God's eye watching me from heaven. Even though I was only twelve years old, I had a strong sense of His Presence with me. I had heard enough sermons that I knew I could call out to God when I was afraid.

All I could say at first in between my sobs was, "God, I'm scared." That is such a common emotion for all of us, isn't it? Being really scared can send our spirit leaping for God to find comfort. I continued my prayer, "I want my father to come back. I don't want my father to leave us, and I especially don't want him to become a woman."

Then I moved on to fill Him in on all the chaos I was dealing with. Obviously, He already knew, but I'd never told Him with deep sobs how I was feeling. "My family is in shambles. My heart is broken. What is taking them so long to get back, Lord?"

Seven o'clock came and went. Then eight o'clock came and went. I was so hungry. This was a time before cell phones, so they had no way to reach me. I kept my eye on that moon believing in my heart it was God's eye watching over me and protecting me. I really got to know God in those five hours of isolation.

That night I made a vow to God that I was determined to honor His instruction found in his Word. In the area of sex, I would remain a virgin until marriage like His Word said. Let me be honest with you, the whole father turning into a woman thing was shameful, perverse, and downright embarrassing.

My father showed up at nine o'clock. He half-heartedly apologized for leaving me there so long. "Time just got away," was the excuse I got. I was so glad to see him that it didn't matter. He had brought pizza and, for that, I was happy.

That night was a turning point for me. I learned that the presence of God was real.

Chapter 5
The Promise to Mom

Mom, too?

Before God started to deal with the pain of my father, another storm severely punctured my sails leaving my life feeling like a ship wrecked and stranded on an abandoned island, much like Tom Hanks was in the 2000 movie, *Castaway*.

This time it was my Mom, my sole provider, the one who stepped up to provide for us when all of life came at her.

Mom, who had been a life-long smoker, was diagnosed with lung cancer at the age of thirty-eight.

A diagnosis like that knocks the wind out of you. I would hear her cry late at night telling God she didn't want to die. I laid on my tear-soaked pillow and wept with her.

One day in the hospital, a chaplain came by to pray with her. He asked my very Catholic mother, if she were to die today, would she go to heaven. She wasn't sure. She had allowed us to go to a Southern Baptist church, but in her heart, she was a devout Catholic. She would have preferred her children to be Catholic, as well. However, she was grateful that her teenagers were in church and making good decisions. I believe she saw the reality of Jesus in our lives. That day, she bowed her head in prayer with that chaplain and prayed the same prayer I had when I was twelve years old. She invited Jesus into her heart to be her Lord and Savior.

Seeing the effects of her losing her hair was devastating to me and painful to look at. Reality was screaming a message loud and clear as to what was happening inside her body. I felt that if I looked away from the large clumps of her hair on the floor that somehow it would all go away.

"What would happen to us if Mom died?" I thought.

My mother was the oldest of seven children, all of whom still lived in New York. She called her baby brother and sister, Artie and Margie, whom she talked about fondly over the years, to ask them for help. My mother was sixteen years old when Artie was born and she loved him just like I did my younger brother, Donny.

She asked my aunt and uncle to take my youngest brother back to New York and raise him because her treatment was not eradicating the cancer. When she told me she had done that, I begged her to let him stay in Arizona. I told her I loved him with all my heart. My mother understood that because she loved Artie the same way. She came up with another plan, but made me promise that I would take care of him if she left him in Arizona.

I gave my mother my word that I would take care of him—a vow that would tear my heart wide open.

Look After the Orphans
She called the pastor of our small Baptist church, Ron Hart, to request a meeting with him. She told him that she was dying and needed homes for her three youngest children: my four-year-old baby brother, my fifteen-year-old sister, and me. I was sixteen.

It wasn't long before we were placed in those homes as we learned the cancer had spread and she had a large tumor growing rapidly on her brain.

I was placed in the home of Neal and Kitchie Julien. I will forever be grateful to them for extending grace, kindness, and godly compassion to my abandoned heart.

I will never forget the day Patty packed up her Ford Pinto with my measly belongings and drove me to their home. She helped me empty my things out of her car. As I stood on that property, watching her tail lights fade from view, I have never felt more alone in this world than I did at that moment. My Rock of Gibraltar was driving away.

I'm going to be honest with you, I walked into their home with a chip on my shoulder. My heart was full of pain. For the most part, I kept it hidden. I was quiet and did what they told me to do.

I was thankful to observe a normal healthy family environment. On most nights, we ate dinner together around the table and had a lot of laughs. A far cry from the environment I left where I was cooking dinner and feeding my brother. All those adult responsibilities were removed from my shoulders.

I was given my own beautiful bedroom, complete with my own bathroom, which was a luxury to me. Kitchie sewed beautiful clothes for me. She was also a hairdresser and cut my hair into cute styles.

She prayed for me. She was a beautiful woman, and she had a kind heart, as did her husband. I became the oldest in their family as her children were only nine and seven years old. Now I knew what it was like to be a middle child, a baby—and in their home, the oldest.

I moved in during the summer when my mother was taken to a nursing home. Before she was moved there, she whispered into my ear once again to take care of Donny. I made a promise to her that I would and that she had nothing to worry about.

The Response

I visited her in that nursing home every day. Before long, she was no longer able to communicate, but I talked to her anyway, not knowing whether she could hear or understand me.

In September, I started college. I was only sixteen years old, but I had started school young. Adjusting to college while watching my mother suffer was a very difficult time in my life.

I had always been a straight-A student. Getting a D in biology that semester was horrible. I found it increasingly difficult to stay focused and concentrate. I never knew from day to day whether it would be her last day.

I will never forget this moment on Thursday, December 13th, 1976. I was at the nursing home talking to my mother like I always did. She usually didn't move or blink, and just laid there while I spoke.

I began to tell her that I would not be stopping by the next day. I was going to one of our college games in Tucson, which was a two-hour drive away.

Suddenly, her arm shot up. Her eyes flicked. It had been months with no response from her. She was trying to tell me something, but what? I figured she was concerned for my safety, so I told her not to worry that I would drive safe and be back to see her on Saturday morning, but Saturday would be too late.

She was trying to say goodbye.

I came home from that game late and went to bed. Two hours later, Kitchie came into my room to tell me that the nursing home had just called; my mom had passed away.

I couldn't believe it had actually happened. Even though the reality was glaringly obvious that she was dying, I still found it hard to believe that she had actually passed.

I was now completely orphaned and alone on the earth. When your parents pass away, it leaves a hole in your heart at any age.

I laid in the bed shocked and tried to envision what she might have been trying to tell me on Thursday. Did she know that she was going to die the next day? I think she did.

I asked the Lord to show me what her final moments were like.

In my spirit, He whispered, 'I came for her myself.' He showed me how He opened the door to her room, the one that I had opened each time I went to see her. He asked her if she was ready to go. She said yes, and He scooped her up into His arms and carried her to heaven. It was so beautiful and soothing to my heart. I thanked God for coming for her and for welcoming her into heaven.

The Promise Tested

Life got back to a new normal, but the promise I made to my mother to look after my baby brother would test my faith at a new level.

The family that took him decided that it would be better for him to never see us again. I cried and pleaded with them. I told them that I had made a promise to my mother that I would take care of him.

I did everything I could and felt it was heartless of them to renege on my mother's signed contract and dying wish to give her children visiting privileges with each other.

I hurt for my baby brother, and I missed him enormously.

Two years went by and the burden of that unfilled promise was eating me up.

When I turned 18 years old, I was of legal age to raise him myself and that promise fueled me.

I cried out to God with deep sobs asking for direction and told Him that I had come to the end of my ability to resolve this issue. I begged Him to appear to me, sit on my bed, and tell me Himself if I was to quit college and raise my brother. I sat there in the dark and shook like a leaf as I fully expected Him to appear.

If He had done what I asked, I would not be here now. I would have died of a heart attack.

Instead of visually appearing, I believed what happened is His Presence came and filled that room. A warmth and a peace so great completely came over me. I stopped crying and nestled into it. God was present! I could feel Him! I wasn't afraid and I wasn't shaking anymore.

In the stillness, the story about Joseph and Benjamin in Genesis 43 filled my mind. Joseph was a teenage boy and had a baby brother, Benjamin, whom he adored. With circumstances out of their control, they were separated for a season, but when that season ended, they were reunited, and the love between them never suffered.

The Lord whispered in the stillness that He wanted me to release my brother for a season, but that He was giving me His Promise that just as Joseph saw Benjamin, I, too, would see my brother again.

My lip began to tremble and I wept deeply. "Lord, how can You ask me to do this? What if he thinks I didn't fight for him and left him?" I cried. "You do realize, Lord, that girls my age are more concerned with what they are going to wear to prom. Why are you making me deal with such hard issues over and over again?"

Nevertheless, the Lord asked me to do a ceremony of sorts to seal this promise. He asked me to find a suitcase and pick a place where I could visualize taking my brother to the Cross. He instructed me to walk towards that makeshift cross, holding my brother's hand in one hand and his suitcase in the other. I was to leave my brother and all of his belongings with the Lord, then turn and walk away without looking back.

Oh, that was hard!

Oh, the bitter tears I wept as the only thing I deeply loved which was still alive, I had to willingly give up.

I wrote a letter to my brother that night and documented exactly what the Lord instructed me to do, and that He had left me with a promise that I will see you one day and that the years we've been apart will be like they never happened. I laminated it the next morning and put it away for safekeeping.

I stopped fretting. I released the burden of the promise I made to my mother to God. God was now working on it and I had confidence that He would not disappoint me.

Chapter 6
The Promise Fulfilled

The Angel Revealed It All

As a child, did you ever do a pinky swear with someone? When God keeps a promise, it far exceeds a pinky swear. When He began to unfold the promise of seeing my brother again thirteen years later, He used fanfare to bring it about.

He sent an angel.

It was Christmas time; my brother was now eighteen years old. My sister had conjured up the idea to find him for me and have him under the tree for Christmas morning with a bright red bow tied around his neck. Nothing would have thrilled me more. I thought about him all the time and I missed him so much.

She kept it top-secret and sent two of her friends to the high school nearest his home to see if anyone knew where he was. They walked around the campus during lunch hour asking students if they knew Donny Jones. All the answers were *no* until they asked the man standing by the bus.

He was dressed in a bus driver uniform, about sixty years old, balding, and with a belly. There was nothing angelic about this man. However, when he was asked the unsolvable question, "Do you know Donny Jones?" The man not only answered, "I sure do!" but also told them his whereabouts for every year we'd been apart from our brother.

They were entirely taken back and replied, "Blond-haired Donny?" and he said, "He had blond hair when he was younger, but now it's dark."

He told them the name of the schools he attended for grade school, junior high, and high school. He explained that my brother had graduated high school mid-year and was getting ready to graduate from Marine Corps Boot Camp in Camp Pendleton.

They told my sister and she began to cry with excitement. She didn't know how to go about checking out his story, so she called me and I put on my private investigator cap once again to see if anything that was said was accurate.

First, I went to the grade school, and sure enough, his picture was in the yearbook. Then, I went to the junior high, and his picture was there, too. I looked closely and was amazed at how he had grown to look just like me. When I went to the high school, I hit a dead end. No one knew him there. So, I called Camp Pendleton and I hit another dead end. They did tell me that if I could get them his social security number, they would be able to look more accurately at their records.

But how was I supposed to get that?

That information miraculously landed in my lap three days later while at a Christmas party after I mentioned my story to a friend. It turns out the social security numbers were also the driver's license numbers at that time. What none of us knew was his first name had been changed from Donny to Matthew. That's why we hit a dead end at the high school and Camp Pendleton. We were asking with the wrong name.

Armed with the new information, I went back to the high school and his senior picture was in the yearbook. My heart began to race as I dialed the phone to speak to the gunnery sergeant at Camp Pendleton. When I heard his voice say, "Hello," I couldn't contain my emotions any longer. I sobbed as I read him the social security number that he needed.

Then he said, "He's here and getting ready to graduate."

I knew the man by the bus was not just a man. He was an angel sent by God to fulfill a promise He had made to my young heart. The man by the bus had answered the question to Donny, not Matthew, and my brother had never ridden the bus once because he only lived around the corner from the school.

The Bible says in Hebrews 13:2 that we can entertain angels and not even be aware of it.

Unbelievable Reunion

I begged the gunnery sergeant for permission to fly out and see my brother. I told him our story of how we had lost our parents and were separated for thirteen years without the privilege of seeing each other. I explained I had all of his baby pictures, which he had never seen. I had made a special book to give to him one day.

The gunnery sergeant stuck his neck out for me, even though he would later tell me everyone in the battalion thought my story seemed fishy. They thought that maybe I was a jilted girlfriend seeking revenge.

I jumped on the first flight to Camp Pendleton. As I sat on that plane, I thought about the night the Lord asked me to trust him and gave me the promise of seeing my brother again. Crocodile tears began to fall down my cheeks. I had no tissue to catch them, so they puddled like raindrops on my lap.

When I arrived at the airport, I rented a car and began the hour-long drive to Camp Pendleton. I tried to envision what it would be like to see my brother again. Would he want to see me? Was he angry that I never contacted him?

Wouldn't you know it, as soon as I arrived, the base was closed to civilians. I had come all that way and had to be turned away.

Not today.

When God is at the helm and it's the appointed time, it's full steam ahead.

The gunnery sergeant, a master sergeant, two drill sergeants, and a staff sergeant all escorted me onto base and took me to a back room of one of their main office tents. They didn't take their eyes off me for a second. I had watched enough military shows to know not to say anything that might incriminate my brother, so I sat there with the photo album on my lap and tried not to engage with them, but they kept talking to me. The master sergeant asked to look at my photo album.

Chapter 7
Healing the Father Wound

The Wound Was Deep

I was a tender child with a soft heart. All I needed for correction was a tilt of the head and a disappointed look from my father, and the tears of repentance would fall. It is important to be aware of the nature of our children's hearts. A tender child does not need the same correction a strong-willed child does.

The damage left upon my heart by my father crushed me in spirit. The discipline I received was too harsh. The Bible warns fathers in particular, in Ephesians 6:4, to not exasperate their children.

The torment of his anger, abuse, and abandonment left my heart broken and repressed in spirit. To survive the pain, I severed that part of my childhood and stuffed it into a closet in my mind, never to be opened again. I figured, out of sight, out of mind. There is no truth to that mentality, but for a time it seemed to halt the pain.

One of the most beautiful things I love about walking with God is that He speaks in the quietness to our soul. In prayer, I heard a knocking. The Lord was asking for permission to enter my room of pain that I'd stored away in my heart. I cast that thought right out of my head as fast as I could. There was absolutely no way that door was going to get opened. I was convinced that pain would swallow me alive if I had to endure it a second time.

God was trying to reach for my pain to heal it, but I was petrified and resisted every attempt He made.

Have you ever felt His knock on the pain of your heart?

The knocking happened over and over again. Months turned into years, and years duplicated into more years; He patiently kept knocking, and I kept resisting. All the while, I carried the weight of the inner turmoil and it was weighing me down, making life so much harder.

I remember one analogy that the Lord gave me in prayer was that of a hiker putting heavy stones in his backpack. These stones represented wounds inflicted upon him. Some of them were boulder-sized and made his journey twice as hard as it should be.

The Lord spoke gently to me, even after years of pursuing me, that by letting Him remove the boulders in my backpack it would lighten my load.

He knew that I carried a great deal of fear and shame along with that pain, which would have to be embraced before turning the doorknob and opening the door for Him.

I had cut off a piece of my own identity. A piece of my inner child was disconnected from my whole person. Psychologically, that is not healthy. I would learn later that a healthy inner child keeps us joyful and embracing life, no matter how old we get.

After years of attempting to reach for my pain in my prayer time, the Lord, out of love, had another plan. He began to reach for my pain during the worship service at church.

Let's Try Something Else
We were invited by a friend to attend her church that worshipped differently than what we knew. At the time, we were attending a Southern Baptist church.

My sister Patty, my comrade in arms, and I decided to sneak into the back of her church one Sunday and check it out. I was full of apprehension walking in there. We sat in the very last pew. I noticed something I didn't see at the Southern Baptist church. These worshippers were singing with their hands raised to the Lord. They tuned out who was to the left and right of them by closing their eyes and singing directly to

God. Even the men worshipped like that and sometimes would weep over their love for God.

Their tears surprised me and made me weep just watching them.

We began attending regularly, but we never moved out of our comfort zone of the last row. We were intrigued, but still glued to our own self-consciousness and spectator mentality.

My sister was actually the first one of us to express an openness to God using her hands. We had both mastered closing our eyes and singing directly to God, but our hands were still at our sides. I glanced at my sister and she had turned her palms up, but her arms were still right by her side. I elbowed her and whispered, "What are you doing? You've completely turned Pentecostal."

We laughed so hard we could hardly catch our breath. As the rest of the church sang the worship songs, we were doubled over in our own Holy Spirit, back-pew moment. We laughed for a long time until we had tears all over our faces. It reminded me of how we had laughed as kids.

It felt like a breakthrough. My tears were releasing part of my fear in understanding this unknown dimension of God.

My work schedule had changed, and I needed to attend the early service by myself. I moved to sitting closer to the front.

I was always more comfortable sitting closer to the front in any meeting where I was not distracted.

As God designed it, His power started reaching for my heart in worship. As I sang and listened to the words, I thought about their meaning and His love, and I literally could not stop crying.

It would last all through worship, week after week. You have to understand, I hardly cried anymore. After going through as much pain as I had, I had simply dried up and thought there were no tears left to cry.

What was really happening was God was allowing me access to my hidden pain in a non-threatening way.

Months later, I started to cry during the sermons, too. One particular sermon, which I don't even remember what he was preaching on, I began to weep so loudly that I couldn't control it.

I was close enough to be disruptive to the sermon and I certainly wasn't trying to be. I will forever be grateful to Pastor Price for not saying anything or drawing attention to my tears. He just continued to preach and allowed God to do the healing He was doing in my heart.

All these tears were draining the infected, impacted pain I had allowed to obstruct my emotions regarding my father. The most rewarding part was that as the pain was draining, God was filling the void with His Love.

The tears were painful to shed, no doubt about it, but it was well worth the feeling of freedom that followed.

After many of these moments, I knew all of these tearful episodes were not just coincidental. God was healing me inside. I began to feel less frightened to let Him in, but there was still much needed healing as fear still had a stronghold on my heart.

As much as I loved God, I was also afraid of Him. I wanted to understand what speaking in tongues was, but I was afraid to get too close to Him to find out.

Receiving My Prayer Language
I was a student at Grand Canyon University in Phoenix, Arizona, which, at the time, was affiliated with the Southern Baptist denomination. One of my friends, who was probably the only non-Baptist student there, told me about a prayer language called the Baptism of the Holy Spirit that strengthened her walk with God.

I had no idea what she was talking about. It seemed just as foreign to me as when Ricki told me God loved me. "How many facets of God's nature are there?" I wondered.

I am sharing this part of my journey, not from a theological standpoint, but as my own experience. Many would disagree with me whether tongues are for today, but I cannot deny how this gift has changed my life.

At a home Bible study with a dear friend and mentor, Vicky, I received the gift of speaking in tongues. I was scared to death, but willing to try.

She gave me a visual to picture myself in a boat and Jesus wanting me to get up and walk to him. That would take faith and trust.

Looking back, it felt more like I was having open heart surgery with no anesthesia.

I had to face my fears and let go of trying to control what I couldn't control. I had to step close enough to God to receive it. I cried the whole time she was praying over me.

"Open your mouth and speak," she encouraged me as I wept.

We waited on God together and she waited on me to overcome my fear of reaching for Him. She was patient with me and I will be forever grateful. I received the baptism of the Holy Spirit that night.

It was quite foreign at first. I found it hard to believe I had it, but I had to open my mouth and use it each day.

What I have learned using my heavenly prayer language now for over forty years, is that there is a power given with this gift to use in prayer that supersedes the flesh.

My flesh wants what it wants, and sometimes my prayer requests can be asked for selfish gain, but when I pray in tongues, I know that I am aligning my will with the will of God.

The stronghold of fear that had held me in bondage for so long was broken with this gift of speaking in my prayer language.

I want everyone to experience the freedom from fear that was given to me.

The authority God has given to me was ignited at a new level. I was able to see that I could take my stand against the powers of darkness, dressed and secured in the armor mentioned in Ephesians 6 to move against the principalities coming against me or others I was praying for.

"Submit to God, resist the devil and he will flee" (James 4:7).

It was like adding a powerful tool to my tool belt as a warrior for the Lord.

In Acts 1:8, when the Holy Spirit came upon His disciples in the upper room, Jesus told them. "You will receive power from on high." The Bible says, in 1 Corinthians 14:2 "For anyone who speaks in a tongue does not speak to people, but to God. Indeed, no one understands them, they utter mysteries by the Spirit."

Oftentimes, when I don't know what to pray, I will use my heavenly prayer language and I know that I am coming into agreement with God's perfect will.

Honor Him Anyway
God had one more step in bringing me complete deliverance to heal me of my "father wound."

He asked me to honor my father.

Exodus 20:12 says, "Honor your father and your mother, so that you may live long in the land the Lord your God is giving you."

I was at a church service where a visiting preacher spoke about all the different roles our parents play in our lives. He had a hat rack with all different kinds of hats on stage with him and used each one as a visual to bring clarity to the importance of honoring one's parents.

At the end of that sermon, there were many at the altar weeping and asking God for forgiveness for not properly honoring their parents. You know where I was? Sitting in the pew thinking that this didn't pertain to me because both of my parents were no longer on the earth.

That night I had a dream wherein the Lord asked me why I hadn't participated. I told Him in my dream that it was because my parents are no longer alive.

He said, "Where in my word does it say to honor them only if they are alive?"

I thought, "It doesn't."

In my dream, I remember telling the Lord, "I don't know how to honor them. They caused a great deal of pain."

He suggested, "How about you honor them for giving you life?"

That I could do.

I jumped out of bed the next morning, ready to do what the Lord suggested. I found a great picture of my parents together and went to Walgreens to have it blown up to 8x10, and bought a frame.

I came home and placed it in a prominent place by the entry of the front door. It became my table of honor for my parents.

Can I be honest with you? It was so strange to see their faces after thirty years of trying to forget. Every time I passed that table, I verbally thanked my father for what he did right. He gave me life, he provided for me, and he loved me to the best of his ability.

Before I knew it, I developed a compassion for the pain he had endured, and it began to flood my heart with an understanding I had lacked.

Honoring my father was more about me. The Lord wanted me to live a long fruitful life, and this was a required step in my journey to joy.

God now had full access to the room beyond the door that He had knocked on for years. He showed me in prayer how I needed to reconnect with the severed inner child for my own health and well-being.

The Lord is patient and slow to anger. He pursues us with His Love, and I am grateful that He never gave up on trying to reach for the pain of my "father wound."

I don't know what weight of pain you are carrying inside, but I want to encourage you to open your heart to God and to not be afraid. He desires to heal you and to bring you into complete freedom and wholeness.

Chapter 8

Creating My Own Family

Up in the Air and Everything

Let me fill you in on a secret that only God and I knew about.

For a year, I prayed for God to bring my future husband into my life. I prayed scripture over him. I prayed for his heart, his job, his relationships, and that God would allow us to meet soon.

I cherished those times with the Lord, and I waited expectantly for Him to lead me to the man of His choosing.

One year later, he showed up at the airport. We were waiting for the same flight. Back then, seats were assigned and we happened to be seated on the same row.

On the plane, he spoke first and we learned quickly that we both attended charismatic churches and were quite involved. The equally-yoked green light went off in my head. That was the most important thing I was looking for in a mate.

Amos 3:3 says, "How can two walk together unless they agree?"

We hit it off and began dating. He was a gentleman and we kept the promise of consummation for marriage according to the boundaries God had ordained.

A year later, we were married.

We welcomed our first child, a son, five years later, and our daughter two years after that.

We were a happy, content family of four.

Life was good.

He was a fantastic provider and a strong entrepreneur. He served our church with passion week after week. He was a loving husband, we did date night on a regular basis, and I was the recipient of lots of flowers.

We built a dream life. I had everything this life could offer and not a financial care in the world as we ran a multi-million-dollar sales business that had him traveling on the road four days out of every week.

God brought us together in a unique way—in an airplane, no less—and as close to heaven as you can get.

- Do I believe that God chose him to be my covering? Yes, I do.
- Do I think He orchestrated our beautiful beginning? Yes, I do.
- Did I marry him? Yes, I did.

Why, then, would God direct me years later to separate what He had joined together?

The Surprise of My Life
Thirty years later, I was praying and reading my Bible one morning when a message dropped into my head seemingly out of nowhere.

"Check his travel computer. Check his web browsing."

I was on a Daniel fast, where I committed to eat only healthy food and drink water for twenty-one days. Because of that, I looked up to God and said, "Just in case that was You, I'll go check it out."

After some fumbling, the room was filled with the hum of his computer.

There, staring back at me, was a history of dating sites being visited regularly.

In utter disbelief, I quickly closed the computer and put it back in his suitcase.

What I didn't know then was that the rest of the iceberg was going to be revealed within hours. Lies that would come slithering out, one by one, from the blackness of their hiding place, to reveal the decomposing secret that would alter the pristine life we had built together.

I confronted my husband with a question I asked him every so often. "How are you doing sexually on the road?"

Emphatically and without glancing away, he looked me straight in the eye and said, "When I am on the road, I am faithful to you. I get my dinner. I go to my hotel room and work on my orders."

He had never given me a reason to question his loyalty or trust before, so I had always taken him at his word. He was firm, adamant, and quite convincing.

I said, "I just looked at your computer and it said you've been looking at dating sites."

He denied it was him. He said someone else must have gotten ahold of his computer. I believed him. I knew he had been with his single brother, and I thought maybe his brother had looked.

We had been going to counseling one day a week for a few months, and that morning we had an appointment. Painful emotions about how he was raised tumbled out of him. Even at fifty-four, he wept as he reminisced over them.

I do believe that men, in general, have a harder time dealing with emotions, so I had been proud of him for looking at some pretty difficult and painful memories of his upbringing.

But when I walked into the counselor's office that morning, I told him I wanted to talk about a new revelation.

My husband just might have fooled me one more time, but the counselor, being persistent and led by the power of the Holy Spirit, did not allow his denial response of, "I don't remember," to go uncontested. He kept pressing back until the truth tumbled out.

When confronted with the truth, I noticed my husband's posture slipped down in his chair until he was slouching and balancing the chair on its two back legs.

He looked like a ten-year-old child trying to avoid taking responsibility. He answered sheepishly showing no emotion or remorse.

The whole escapade of, "I looked at dating sites," could have ended right then and there and I would have gone home none the wiser.

But our counselor was an expert at getting to the truth. After further questioning, my husband divulged more information that took him from "looking" at dating sites to actually "having" multiple dating profiles.

That lead to the breakthrough question, "How did the ladies contact you?"

Without blinking, he responded, "I have a secret email."

I said, "I wanted to look at that right now."

What I saw, I would not wish on my worst enemy. He had created not one, not two, but five dating site profiles portraying himself as a cool California single man, never married, with no children. On all of them, he said he had a college degree, which he does not.

He had three alias names, each one carefully crafted by changing only one letter in his last name. It would be very easy to call it a typo should anyone catch onto him. Each alias said he was from a different city in California. Each one had him at a different age, much younger than the age he actually was. He posted bright all-American smiling photos of himself. His profile was written from the perspective of a fun-loving, romantic man looking for his soul mate. By all accounts, he looked like a great catch.

Next, we looked at the responses in his inbox. There were over 400 women. All of them were Filipino. There were full chat room conversations complete with webcam nudity and sexual experiences. Hundreds of emails with photos of naked bodies begging him to send them money so they could buy their children medication.

I scrolled down and scrolled down until I came to the end of the inbox messages.

I got a sick tightening sensation in my stomach.

There, screaming back at me was a date that read ten years earlier.

I looked at him in shock that any of this could possibly be true.

He was still slouched down in his chair and now rocking on the two back legs. Oblivious. Emotionless. Relieved. His secret was out. The reality of his two worlds had collided.

He had built an empire, deceiving himself, first, then deceiving me and his children. Lastly, deceiving and manipulating hundreds of women for his own personal pleasure.

How does a loving husband and good provider go from that role to a deviant sexual predator?

It didn't happen overnight, that's for sure.

"I'm Leaving"
Just like that, he said, "I'm going to tell the kids I've been living a double life, and I'll be leaving tonight."

He was completely disconnected from the reality of his behavior. His ability to pull off this master manipulation scheme for ten years and compartmentalize it all was truly a scene out of a movie.

We sat down as a family for the meeting.

He looked like he was celebrating his big reveal while eating a banana split from Dairy Queen.

With his mouth full of ice cream, he spat out, "I've been living a double life and I'm moving out tonight."

Ruthless and still showing zero signs of remorse, his voice contorted as he responded in a tone that wasn't even his own. When the kids asked him if he had other wives and children, he replied sheepishly, "Why are you being so mean to me?"

At that moment, I stared at him, utterly shocked.

He just sucker-punched both of his children in their guts and all he could think about was his next bite of banana split.

I did not recognize the man sitting across from me. He was not my husband. He finished his ice cream and got up and left. My world, as I knew it, exploded.

The days ahead would continue to arrest my heart with nightmarish revelations, emotional upheavals, and dark days of the soul. The depravity and shock would collide with my emotions and the shut-off valve to my tears would become locked in the open position.

Nothing was gained from what he exchanged and it resulted in empty pockets and an empty life that cost him everything.

He created a dichotomy, a world of its own that first took up space in his imagination. It became a place of escape where he hid for years. All the while, he had continued to work and provide for our family. The distancing was subtle. Quietly, without us knowing what he was doing, he would add one more day on the road. He used the excuse that he was drumming up more money for business, when in reality, he was building an empire of women who were no longer harmless images on a screen; now they were affairs with real women with flesh and blood.

Later I would learn from him that God had given him multiple opportunities to turn from his secret life during those ten years. When he had purposed in his mind to make our marriage work, while simultaneously continuing to live the secret lifestyle that he was entrenched in, God stepped in and said, "Your time is up; this is my daughter."

My husband was a good man who slowly followed the forbidden intoxicating path of sexual sin so warned about in Proverbs. Every day, he went deeper and deeper into the thrill of it, until the cliché, "He sold his soul to the devil," became his reality.

What happened to him could happen to anyone, including me. Temptation is creeping all around us. We have to guard our hearts and have a plan before it presents itself.

Little did he know when he first started dabbling in this secret sin of pornography that he entered a slippery slope that would cost him everything.

Ted Bundy was an American serial killer who kidnapped, raped, and murdered more than eighty young college women during the 1970's. After more than a decade of denial, he confessed to only thirty of those homicides.

He left America with an eye-opening interview right before he was executed for his sexual crimes.

He told the world that his deviancy started with viewing pornography. He further stated that every man he has shared the prison system with had an addiction to pornography.

I believe many good men who are addicted to pornography don't think the habit will alter their brains or change them to become violent. On the contrary, Ted Bundy thought the same thing. Even he never thought he would become "Ted Bundy, the serial killer." It happens. It is a slippery slope that, as Proverbs warns us, will lead down the path to death.

You can watch his testimony on YouTube under "Ted Bundy last interview with Dr. James Dobson."

Being on the backside of this, I am overwhelmed at the love of God to step in and reveal the truth to me when I had no idea that I was being held hostage in my own home.

I hope that if you are reading this book and are caught up in sexual sin that you run from it and go find help. It is not worth the misery to yourself or to your family.

It was a long journey for me to find wholeness again in my soul.

Chapter 9

Broken Beyond Repair

How Do I Come Back from That?

It is the mastery of God to have developed a grieving process for our emotions in times of trauma. It gave me a coping mechanism that helped me absorb the trauma, as I was in shock and disbelief that this was my new reality.

The remaining phases of anger, bargaining, depression, and acceptance would come much later.

In my shock, I couldn't sleep, I couldn't eat. I couldn't cry. I was in a zombie-like state of mind.

I didn't chase him. I didn't call him. I didn't initiate any contact with him. I couldn't think clearly. I felt frozen in time.

When I began to thaw out, two throbbing questions gnawed at me. The first one was, had he actually slept with any other women?

I didn't want to consider that thought because, if he had, I knew I could have potentially been given a transmitted disease.

The other throbbing question that wouldn't go away was, how did I miss this?

I played out scenarios in my mind, searching for clues from previous conversations.

What added insult to injury was the beautiful evening of sexual intimacy we'd had together less than twenty-four hours earlier.

After seven days of no contact, I finally mustered up the courage to call and ask him the formidable question I was wrestling with.

"I want to know if you slept with anyone."

Complete silence.

Finally, he spoke. "I don't want to hurt you."

My response was, "You should have thought of that a long time ago."

So, I asked him again, letting him know my concern about transmittable diseases.

His response, "Well, I don't have any, so you shouldn't either."

I asked a third time and finally got an answer.

"Yes," he said.

"How many?"

"Six."

I asked him, "Why did you play this charade? If you wanted this lifestyle, why didn't you leave me?"

"Because I love you," he said.

I said, "This is not love."

Silence.

I've never been physically stabbed with a knife, but that night my heart felt the iron blade of betrayal so deep that my emotions bled profusely.

I was completely caught off-guard by this crass maneuver.

Where was the kind and caring man I knew as my husband? One day he was here, and the next he wasn't.

Not only had our marriage been attacked, but our business and livelihood were showing signs of stress and decline.

When God Hides You in Chaos
Six months prior to his double life coming to light, my husband led us to file Chapter 13 bankruptcy. I didn't want to do this. I felt we should pay what we owed, no matter how long it took.

Drowning in a sea of debt, he felt this would wipe the slate clean and we could rebuild. As much as I hated it, I followed his leadership.

What I didn't know was that God, in all His wisdom, put me smack in the eye of this bankruptcy storm and said, "Trust me!"

When God sets you in the eye of any storm, it is actually the safest place you can be. Though the chaos swirls around you, there is a sustainable peace in the eye of the storm.

Emotions were raging in our home. My husband was caught in a convoluted mess of his own making and we were all trying to survive the destruction he had created.

My son, who was twenty-four years old, begged his father to open his eyes and walk away from the darkness that was pulling him down the wrong path. My daughter, twenty-two, was angry and wanted nothing to do with her father.

I had lost fifteen pounds because I was still writhing in shock. I couldn't eat. My body couldn't sleep. I was swimming in a pool of uncertainty. What if I had contracted a disease?

I was a complete mess when I had my blood drawn to face the formidable question, "Had he infected me with a disease?"

The bloodwork came back clear. No evidence of transmitted diseases.

I've heard the phrase, "What God starts, He finishes." God has started this journey to rescue me, not to cause me unbearable pain, although pain was going to be a part of the long treacherous journey back to wholeness. It seemed to swallow me up and I felt I would have a permanently altered emotional limp and never be able to return to being my sweet joyful self.

How do we trust God within the deep ache of pain?

The one thing I had going for me was that I knew my identity in Christ. My faith was mine, and my whole life up until this point had resonated it back to Him as my gift. Would I believe Him this time, just as He had walked with me before? At this moment in my journey, I wanted to believe Him, but the despair in my heart and the feeling of being permanently crippled was agonizing.

I reached back to remember all the things that God had walked me through, things that gave me something to cling to so that my faith could climb up on top of these intense emotions and dare to believe God anyway.

I'm going to leave you hanging on this story for a few chapters and take you back to a season where God actually built the faith I would need to heal from this experience.

Chapter 10

Facts or Faith?

Prayerful Beginning

I am a firm believer that, though a man and a woman do their part in the procreation process, new life will always be a gift from God. The miraculous weaving of intricate body parts inside a womb that sustains a person for a lifetime is the Designer of creation doing His finest work in secret.

We decided to start our family five years into our marriage, but it wasn't happening as fast as I wanted it to and it deeply grieved me. My arms felt empty and I longed for a baby to fill them.

Has your heart ever been plagued with a longing unfulfilled?

Maybe it wasn't for a baby; maybe you wanted to get married, or you were overlooked for a promotion at work. When a longing lingers in the heart, words cannot adequately convey the hidden pain that others may never understand.

I found immense comfort from the story of Hannah in 1 Samuel 1. She also desired a baby and was not getting pregnant. She also had a time with not being able to control her emotions. I love what she did. She went to God with her request. She laid out her desire before the only One who could fulfill her request.

I followed her example.

I interceded and asked God for a son and said that I would also dedicate him to God as Hannah did with her first-born, Samuel.

I stayed in that posture of prayer even when months continued to pass with no signs of pregnancy.

One Sunday, in April of 1989, we had a woman by the name of Cindy Jacobs visit our church. She heads up a ministry called Generals International. At the end of her sermon, she asked people to join her at the altar if they wanted prayer. I made my way to the platform and stood with many others as she started to pray over each life, starting from the left and moving to the right. I was somewhere in the middle of the lineup. She used words over every other person, but when she came to me she did something unique.

She blew on me without saying one word.

I went to the doctor that week and learned I was pregnant. I remember dropping to my knees as I hung up the phone and I wept with gratitude. I thanked God deeply for allowing me the privilege of becoming a mother.

The Lord gave me clear instructions that I was to intercede for the child I was carrying at the altar of my church for the entire nine months of my pregnancy. To stay accountable, I asked a friend of mine to join me since she was carrying her first child, as well, and together, we prayed for the children we would soon deliver.

On my due date, my husband and I were at a church service listening to a visiting prophet Dick Mills speak. He had a prophetic gift, and he called us out and asked us both to come up to the front. I waddled up there with my great big belly and he gave me this word, "Everything the child you are carrying needs is already bought and paid for. No matter what it looks like, whether the earth gives way or a tsunami rises in the sea, this child is bought and paid for."

He turned to my husband and said, "This woman is a gift to you. Her heart is a garden. As long as you tend to it and water it, it will produce a bounty for you."

* * *

Nothing, and I mean nothing, has ever beaten Christmas for me. I was the child who tried to stay awake to catch Santa eating the cookies we left for him. I loved decorating the yard and the tree and making handmade gifts in school to give my parents.

As an adult, I added a Hallmark romance movie, a hot cup of cocoa, and being wrapped up in a warm blanket and snuggling by a warm fire. Now, that was Christmas at its finest.

However, if I stacked up every Christmas I'd ever had, none of them would add up to the anticipation and excitement I felt when I was about to deliver my first child.

The day of birth finally arrived, albeit two weeks past the due date. Once my water broke, they realized that the baby had a meconium aspiration in the womb—basically, his first bowel movement. These toxins were now inside of me, causing a high fever and vomiting.

Labor was scary enough as I wrestled with the fear of the unknown. I had nothing to compare it to, but experiencing flu-like symptoms while simultaneously having intense contractions was exhausting, mentally and physically. The hours seemed to drag by and I could not see the end in sight.

After thirty-six hours, I had finally transitioned. As they propped my feet in the stirrups to start pushing, I was delirious with exhaustion and sobbing for relief. I had no strength. If they had told me then that I would be pushing for the next four hours, I might have collapsed thinking it was just too much.

It was game on.

This baby needed to be born safely, and it was up to me to make that happen. Now I understood why God had me pray beforehand. This was so hard.

I watched as seven NICU specialists lined up at my feet watching for the baby's arrival. All of them had life-saving instruments in their hands.

After four strenuous hours of pushing, my son was finally born. He came out a fighter. As they held him up, his arms and fists were in a position of a warrior. They whisked him away quickly to save his life. He was immediately put on antibiotics and monitored closely.

He was the biggest baby in the NICU at eight pounds, two ounces. Most of the newborns were "premies;" he looked like a giant next to them. I didn't know the extreme condition my son was in. I had just given all I had and was completely out of it.

I was still throwing up after he was delivered, so I was started on antibiotics for the meconium in my womb, as well. We both had a longer hospital stay, but miraculously this event that could have taken both of our lives didn't.

Intuition of a Mother

We named him Justin, and he grew to be a strong-willed little guy, but loving and obedient. He would wake up at the crack of dawn, ready to start his day with gusto. He loved to play in the dirt out in the backyard. We created a place for him to dig and play with his trucks. He built bridges with his Legos and I marveled at how smart he was. He somehow knew to put four pieces on each side to make his bridge level.

I realized he was a visual learner early on. When it came time to introduce him to his ABCs, I took popsicle sticks outside and played with him in the dirt. The truck would transport the sticks and then he would make an A or an E or F with them. I had to really work on the other letters that curved, but he finally got it.

On Saturday morning, right before his second birthday, his dad and I were having breakfast at the kitchen table. As usual, he was outside playing at his pile of dirt. Everything in the back was protected for him. The pool was fenced in. The gates were locked. He came into the house and said in his toddler language, "Me fink nake."

At first, I didn't pay attention to him, but after doing my mother-interpretation in my mind, I asked him to say it again. It sure sounded to me like he said, "Me think snake." I told him to take me outside and show me.

To my horror, coiled up within twelve inches of where he had been playing, was a large, sleeping Mojave rattlesnake—the deadliest of all rattlesnakes. Once again, his life was spared.

Before we knew it, it was time to get him registered for kindergarten. Grace Community Christian School in Tempe, Arizona was our first choice, but there was a new student waiting list. That sent me praying for a spot to open up for him. I saw they needed a Moms in Touch leader for a Moms prayer group for the school. I told God that if He would get Justin in, I would step up and lead that group. He opened up a spot for Justin, and I did what I promised.

Moms in Touch is a prayer initiative created for mothers to pray for their children and other students during the educational process. I led this for five years with a group of other mothers who were committed to meeting once a week and praying for the children. When Justin was in fifth grade, another mother took the lead, but I remained in the group.

During these years, I felt a bond with each of these young students in the school, praying that the plans God had for their lives would come to pass. I prayed for the vocation they would enter into as their chubby cherub cheeks sang in Christmas pageants. They continued to grow and develop as each year rolled into the next. I saw more and more of their unique giftings and personalities become clearer as they grew. These students would make a difference in this world and I was honored to bow my knee on their behalf. God gave me a love for each one of them that I still have today.

Experts say that a mother's intuition is one of the strongest premonitions known to humanity and should always be trusted. Sometimes a mother will have knowledge of something without proof, evidence, or understanding of where that knowledge came from. I think all mothers will experience this phenomenon at least once when raising their children.

I had one on February 11th, 2003, when Justin was thirteen years old. He had a bad cold and was on day three of staying home from school.

During my spin class at the gym, something inside of me told me to get home right away, that something was not right with Justin. I listened to it and left early.

When I got there, a neighbor who was an emergency room doctor stopped over and noticed a rash had formed on his back. She called it "petechiae" and seemed very concerned and said we needed to get to the hospital.

She called ahead to the emergency room she worked at to let them know we would be coming in. She met us there, even though it was her day off. I had no idea what the concern was, but they all seemed to be moving quickly with a hushed tone.

Two hours later, I would learn from our neighbor that my son didn't have just a sinus infection, he had a fatal form of leukemia, a disease that dries up the bone marrow and does not allow it to reproduce healthy red and white blood cells and platelets.

I looked straight into the eyes of this loving and caring friend and neighbor who was trained for moments like this. I tried to read her. I was speechless while she was professional and poised. She was the exact person God had chosen for this moment. I did not hear this news from a stranger. I heard it from a friend.

"Your son has cancer."

My first words to her were, "Is he going to die?"

Of course, she handled that with grace, but she also knew time was of the essence. She told me only the bare basics I needed to know at that moment. He was rushed to Phoenix Children's Hospital via ambulance as my numb body followed behind in my car.

They would need to do further testing to determine which of the four types of leukemia he had.

My mind raced.

Pastors met us down at the hospital. Prayers were prayed over all of us as many helped us shoulder the devastating news. Tears were shed by all. We learned all too soon that Justin had the most severe form of leukemia, AML.

This type can cause death within two weeks. Typically, even with aggressive chemotherapy, most survive for four to six months after diagnosis. He'd already been sick for a week. Would he even survive the night?

Students came and were shell-shocked as they looked at Justin lying in the bed with his pale white skin screaming back at them. His bone marrow was sick unto death.

Death was not something seventh-grade students thought about with their peers. They may have experienced the death of a grandparent. That seemed like the natural course of events after a life well-lived, but not to a thirteen-year-old. This stopped everyone in their tracks and made us all think long and hard about the depth of our own lives and how we treated each other.

After a long day at the hospital, I went home to comfort our daughter as my husband stayed with Justin through the first night.

What Do You See?
People live their lives with many different outlooks. Some adopt the "que sera, sera" approach and believe that what is meant to be will just be; we're just supposed to sit back and let things happen, and the faster we accept it the easier it will be to swallow.

The dichotomy of the facts colliding with my faith made the mother-bear intuition of fight rise up within me. I couldn't sit back and watch my son die without doing something.

I stayed up all night thinking, pacing, praying, and folding laundry in between to keep my nervous energy occupied.

I went through every scenario of how this could have happened. I remember saying to God, "I prayed for his life from even before his birth as You instructed me to. You healed him at birth. Why did You not protect him from getting this?"

Up until that moment, I had believed that my prayers were building a wall of protection around my children so that no evil would come near

Chapter 11
Wading in the Waiting

Aggressive Treatment

Without warning, we were displaced from what was our so-called normal life and dumped into a hospital setting that felt a bit like a concentration camp. Withering bodies lingered from disease leaving them looking like survivors from the Holocaust.

Albeit at the strike of every minute, one would lose their battle as others looked on hoping they were not next in line.

Time continued to march on, but the nagging question we all dared not verbalize was, will time continue to march on for Justin?

IV poles, beeps, monitors, bald heads, and weeping parents were the daily grind. The aggressive treatment to bring his bone marrow counts down to kill the leukemic cells required an entire six months in the hospital.

They warned us that with this particular treatment, his body could spontaneously shut down and that was why he needed to remain in the hospital.

He required constant blood transfusions to replace the good cells that were being destroyed alongside the bad ones.

I came to understand that the blood donations of strangers were keeping him alive. Have you ever donated your blood? You may never know the story of how your donation saved a life, so let me tell you from the bottom of my heart, thank you!

Those donations just seemed to show up right when we needed them.

Except for when they didn't.

One morning, he woke up to internal bleeding somewhere in his body. They didn't know where it was coming from, and without a donation of coagulating platelets, he could bleed to death.

There were no platelets in the blood banks that day. My team of prayer warriors prayed that God would spare his life providing platelets, and God answered.

Late in the afternoon, someone donated those cells and ultimately saved his life. His bleeding ceased.

We won this battle, but the war waged on.

Praise Your Way Through It
Cancer waits for no one to catch up. The fiery assaults of death threats are assailed one after another on your mind, body, spirit, and emotions.

Watching my son suffer and not be able to stop it was taking its toll on me. I saw the pain of other patients and the grief in the faces of their parents. Little children were dying in their arms. It was the deepest and saddest pain I have ever witnessed.

It was difficult for marriages to survive the ongoing trauma of the lengthy decline of their child. I saw husband and wives separate. I saw affairs take place between the parent of one child and the parent of another child. The stress was enormous.

It is very difficult to find comfort in the arms of your spouse when they're barely trying to keep their head above water themselves. My husband still shouldered the pressure to provide for us. I would do the dayshift, and after work, he would come and do the night shift. We did what we had to do to get our family through this ordeal.

I could tell as the days went one after another and then turned into months on end, that my husband was distancing himself. During the platelet scare, he went to an eBay seminar to learn how to sell products online. I begged him to not go and stay with me that day. I will admit, it was getting harder and harder for both of us to keep showing up. The reality of Justin passing that day was high, but he left me there alone to deal with it by myself and went to that seminar.

I shed a lot of tears that day, but I learned that I had to stay with God no matter how I felt and no matter what anyone else did. My son was fighting to live, and I would fight right alongside him.

Worship and prayer were my battle cry. It was what I did all day long. I sat at his bedside praying and worshipping for hours as he slept. He could hear me and it gave him great comfort. He had a deep faith even then, and a faith that rose above any fear.

At thirteen years old, Justin was barely a teenager, yet I was amazed at his resolve.

One of the songs that I played over and over on my drive to and from the hospital— and sometimes through the night—was "You Are God Alone," by Phillips, Craig, and Dean from their 2004 album, *Let the Worshippers Arise*. This is a contemporary Christian worship trio: Randy Phillips, Shawn Craig, and Dan Dean. All of them are gifted musicians and serve as pastors.

The message is about an unchanging God who was on His throne before time began, ruling and reigning in good times or bad. The lyrics to that song gave me stability when everything in my world was anything but stable.

One of the doctors, an older man named Dr. Baranko, took a special interest in Justin. He was going to retire when we arrived on the scene, but for some reason, he stayed. I could tell the years had etched a hard crusty exterior onto him. I completely understood why. He had given his life to pediatric oncology and lost more than he saved.

He would invite Justin out to the unit desk when he was working, and he'd talk with him, man to man. He'd tease him saying that, when this was all over, they'd go out for a drink somewhere. He kept Justin in the fight. I could tell his heart was guarded, but he still cared.

What's Happening?

I arrived at the hospital like every other day. Justin said he wasn't feeling well. Within five minutes, every doctor ran into his room. They began to do what they are trained to do in an emergency situation with precision.

Justin's body was shutting down. He had gone into sepsis. Time was of the essence. He was placed on a stretcher and rushed to the ICU. They were running and pumping fluids into his body. Everyone was moving fast.

They had warned us that his vitals could shut down this fast. Justin had befriended a male intern a few weeks before this. It turned out that this young man was a Christian and Justin talked to him in-depth about God and healing many times when he came to visit him.

That intern was running alongside his stretcher. I knew that, figuratively speaking, he had removed his doctor coat and was interceding for Justin as a fellow brother in Christ. Justin yelled his name and said, "Pray!"

Justin began to speak in tongues loudly. I'd never heard him speak in tongues before. I knew the Holy Spirit was hovering over him and praying through him.

He was immediately put on a ventilator to keep his body stabilized because on the way to ICU they were pumping massive amounts of fluid into his body to stabilize his vital organs. His lungs took a big chunk of that. We would have to wait to see if his lungs could dissolve it or if pneumonia would set in.

I kept thousands of people who were following our story updated and asking for prayer on our blog.

Just Tell Me

I remember pleading with God, over and over again, to just tell me whether Justin would live or if he was going to die. I was exhausted from living day to day, not knowing the final outcome.

Would my faith be different if I knew? Would your faith be different if you knew the final outcome of a crisis you were in?

The Lord let me ask Him many times, and then He said, 'I don't want you to ask me that again.'

He led me to a verse in Psalm 131:2 that tells of a weaned child who, sitting next to his mother, is content.

He reminded me of the exasperation my infants had experienced when they were trying to latch onto my breast for nursing. They had worked themselves up to an agitation and couldn't calm down even though the provision was right there.

In this verse, this same suckling child now sits peaceably beside the same provision that was used to sustain him.

No restlessness, but a calm composure!

The Lord was asking me to let Him carry the answer to my question. What He was more interested in was that I would trust Him completely, even in the 'not knowing.' He had the provision I needed and would give it to me at the time I needed it.

He wanted me to find a strength in my core to sit with no restlessness and with a strength inside that believed He would lead me through this no matter what the outcome would be.

Have you ever experienced a weary traveling toddler asking over and over, "Are we there yet?" They don't see the mileage required for the journey. All they see is the landscape from the window in the backseat.

Isn't that response like most of us when we want to know the final outcome of our prayers? God was building my faith to walk in peace even in the unknown and to not question Him every five minutes of what, when, how, and why. I learned to sit at peace in my spirit and to put my focus on Him, and I let Him hold the provision and the answer.

It wasn't an easy lesson to learn, but nonetheless, when I finally stopped resisting the awkward uncomfortable place of not knowing, a life-changing mind shift happened for me.

I learned to sit calmly next to the One who held all my answers.

The Second Breath
Cindy Jacobs was back in the Phoenix area and was invited to come pray for him. Guess what she did?

She blew on him.

Within days, Justin was completely fine. In fact, he was up and walking around the corridor with his friends and I heard a page calling him back to his bed. Not many ICU patients get up and can't be found. God had come through.

I have no idea what the breath was all about, but I recalled the night Justin was first diagnosed and the Lord told me to hang onto Ezekiel 37:4-10

> Then he said to me, "Prophesy to these bones and say to them, 'Dry bones, hear the word of the LORD! This is what the Sovereign LORD says to these bones: I will make breath enter you, and you will come to life. I will attach tendons to you and make flesh come upon you and cover you with skin; I will put breath in you, and you will come to life. Then you will know that I am the LORD.'"
>
> So I prophesied as I was commanded. And as I was prophesying, there was a noise, a rattling sound, and the bones came together, bone to bone. I looked, and tendons and flesh appeared on them and skin covered them, but there was no breath in them.
>
> Then he said to me, "Prophesy to the breath; prophesy, son of man, and say to it, 'This is what the Sovereign LORD says: Come, breath, from the four winds and breathe into these slain, that they may live.'" So I prophesied as he commanded me, and breath entered them; they came to life and stood up on their feet—a vast army.

I remembered that I did not have to understand it all; I just had to trust that God did, and that was good enough.

The war still raged on as this was just another hill we had climbed. There was still no end in sight. All we could do was face each day as it presented itself.

After that event, his initial treatment was over and Justin was found to be in remission. It had been an eighteen-month journey. He returned to school for eighth grade looking strong, rugged, and handsome.

Life got simpler, and we welcomed the reprieve. He would have regular checkups to watch his blood counts. Everything looked good until one day when it looked questionable. A bone marrow biopsy was scheduled to make sure. Unfortunately, it came back as positive. The only treatment left was a bone marrow transplant.

The NFL Player
Have you ever felt like you were making progress on something going up the ladder three steps only to be knocked down five?

It is a discouraging and defeating feeling. We felt like we were starting all the way over.

I didn't want my son to suffer anymore, but I couldn't stop it.

God knew how hard this was going to be, and he laid it on the heart of a young man who heard our story on the news to come visit Justin.

He walked into our hospital room and into our lives armed with a strength our whole family would need.

He was a handsome young man who had played NFL football. His name was Damon Dunn. Damon played wide receiver for the Cleveland Browns in 1999 and the New York Jets in 2000. He also played with the Jacksonville Jaguars in 1998 and the Dallas Cowboys in 2001 during their off-seasons.

I loved his passion right away. He came in with his Bible in his hand and he began to preach and tell us all the strategy he learned in football on how to overcome and win. He said, "When challenges are present, you rise to the occasion."

He was an answer to my silent prayers. I had prayed, "Lord, I'm getting tired. This is so hard." It was just three days later that this ball of fire came to us.

No matter what life presents to us, God will provide the tools and community to make it through. We never walk alone. We were made to be in community with each other. He has divine connections everywhere. If you are seeking Him and praying and asking for direction, He will give you all you need to make it through your situation.

Not only was Damon full of wisdom, but he was also hilarious and kept us in stitches. The Lord says in Proverbs 17:22 that laughter is good medicine. With Damon around, the Lord was supplying us with ample doses of His kind of medicine. Most importantly, he was there to get Justin ready for the biggest game of his life.

But first, a donor had to be found.

They told us that it would be a one-in-six-million chance that another human being on this earth would match him. They tested each of us in our family, and we were not a match. I learned so much about the six main markers of DNA. Three are given to us by our mother and three by our father. The other remaining markers, (there are ten, total) are random and coincidental to each sibling.

Our church held a large bone marrow drive. It was very well done, and we had a huge turnout. It was like looking for a needle in a haystack. People lined up to have their finger pricked and a sample of their blood taken. Interestingly, bone marrow is not the same as blood matching.

Unfortunately, not one of them was a match for Justin. Years later, we learned that more than fifteen of those who submitted samples that day went on to become a donor for someone else. Once you are in the bone marrow registry, your sample remains.

On Thanksgiving Day of 2005, we received a call that a donor match had been found. All we were told was it would be coming from a 32-year-old woman.

Thanksgiving Day took on a new meaning.

A Gift from a Stranger
The plan was to bring Justin as close to death as they could and then bring him back to life. He would experience a rebirth, as they called it, if all

went according to plan. We had to sign waivers that made my maternal heart bleed profusely. Signing those forms, knowing the side effects and possible sentence of death, was almost too much to bear.

I knew I was not in control of my child's life—God was. These are the moments when I stepped into a faith I did not know I had. I was being thrust into it. I had to step up or be taken out. I chose to step up. I would continue to fight alongside my son. Once the counts were low, Justin would endure twelve rounds of full-body radiation. It grieved me deeply to know what he was to endure.

Damon became a coach to him. He explained to Justin that he would be taking the field of radiation, just like when he took the NFL field. He said, "No matter what field we're on, we play to win. We never let our guard down, no matter who is in the lead. The game is always won in the last three seconds of the game."

I will always be thankful to Damon for these nuggets of truth he generously shared with our family. He wheeled Justin to most of those appointments. He made sure Justin had fun along the way, pretending the wheelchair was a racecar and popping wheelies.

But, when the huge door of the radiation room opened, both of them had their game face on. This is what Damon had trained him for. This was why all the laughs were had. This was game time.

We all knew this was a 'win or lose on the field' situation.

Justin stood with his arms tied out as if he were on a cross. I couldn't help but remember who else had hung like that, and the sacrifice of Jesus as he hung on the cross for our sins and for Justin's healing.

As Justin stood and endured the treatment, Damon stood on the outside looking through the window with his firm game face. In those moments, I envisioned Damon dressed in his football gear complete with the helmet and black marks under his eyes. Damon was a survivor, himself. He came from poverty and a single-parent family. He learned about the love of God and how to live his life to please Him. He had used all the principles in the Bible to create success in his own life, and here he was, paying it forward to a stranger God told him to help.

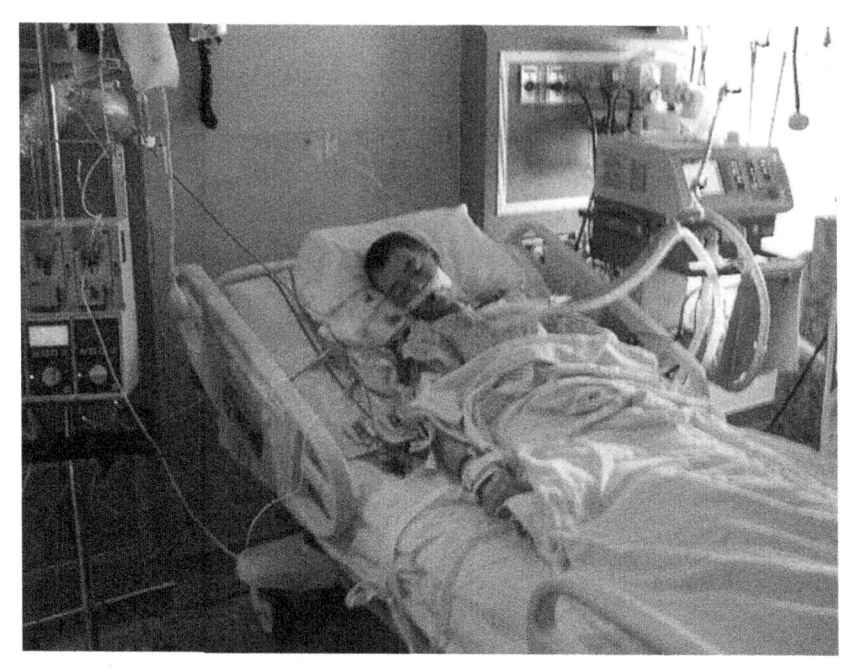

Justin got very sick after all the treatment and held on until the bone marrow cells arrived. When I saw the team of eight enter the room carrying the red igloo labeled "organ donation," I thought of movies I'd seen where a liver or heart transplant organ was delivered to a dying patient.

His two friends, Joey and Brad, were in the room at the time. They had been good friends supporting Justin during this very difficult journey. I asked if I could pray over the bag and you would have thought I'd asked to step into the President's chambers.

This was definitely outside of protocol. However, all of them circled around Justin's bed as I bellowed out a heart-wrenching prayer of gratitude to the Lord. I blessed the donor and asked for these cells to successfully take inside of Justin's body.

Everyone was crying. It was such a powerful moment. The bag was hung in silence as we stood watching it drip into his dry bones, praying this was the long-awaited answer.

I thought about the donor. I didn't know who she was or what she'd had to endure to give her cells to Justin. I wanted so badly to tell her, "Thank you," but they said I had to wait a year before even trying to contact her.

The days that followed were the hardest he had to endure and the hardest for me to watch. He developed graft vs. host disease, which is something they said was good in a small dose. It's when the donor cells fight with the patient's own cells as to which immune system will take over. He developed painful mouth ulcers, abdominal pain with vomiting, fevers, and rash. The staff did what they could to make him comfortable, but a constant fentanyl drip was necessary to reduce the pain.

Christmas Day at the hospital was by far the hardest Christmas I have ever had to endure. My son was in so much pain. There was no tinsel, no tree, no presents, no family feast, no laughter.

I sat in the dark at his bedside on a stool, held his hand, and prayed non-stop as the tears rolled down my cheeks. Before Dr. Schriber left for the day, he peeked into our room. There was nothing he could do to take away the pain, but I could see the look of compassion on his face.

His transplant procedure was done at an all-adult hospital, whereas his treatment before had been done at Phoenix Children's Hospital. There was something called Child Life at the children's hospital. Child Life specialists are trained to engage the child exactly in the way they are wired to keep them in the fight. Sometimes, they'll do a puppet show in their room or draw a picture with them. They were always cheerful and brought much fun to Justin. He was not able to leave his room, so he looked forward to these daily visits. I suppose it was psychology in disguise.

We were missing them right about now, and I didn't realize what an important role they played. Personally, I believe that adults would benefit from the program, as well. But, now was not the time for that. Justin was despairing. Damon was not available. I did my best to stay with him, but the staff recognized that he was withdrawing.

Days turned from one into the next, and he had fought so hard and so long. If he didn't turn around, they were considering placing him into a care facility. I explained to them about Child Life. These doctors were not great with bedside manner. They had an enormous patient load with serious life-threatening issues.

Death happens every day for these doctors, and the less they are engaged, the less it hurts. Justin was only fourteen years old. One doctor went above and beyond his normal routine. He came into Justin's room one day and asked him to show him how to play one of his race car videos. Mind you, this doctor really had no desire to play this video game. But when he saw Justin sit up in his bed and grab a remote and the doctor sat down in the chair and Justin handed him the other remote, something happened. He had reached Justin. He had pulled him out; something none of the others doctors were able to do. I will be forever grateful to him for his efforts. He tried something out of his normal and it worked.

Justin began to recover after that and was finally able to go home. For months, we had regular visits from homecare that helped in areas he needed help.

During all of his treatments in the hospital, I was also his homeschool teacher. He completed most of his assignments the school gave him in a timely manner and would turn them in. On the days he wasn't feeling well, they allowed more time. Because of this arrangement, he was caught up with his class. The same students that had started kindergarten with him were the same students I had prayed over in Moms in Touch.

These same students were a praying force that carried Justin through. We did it as a community. These parents served and cared, and their kindness will never be forgotten. Many took care of my daughter. Many cooked meals. There was a website blog that one family hosted and that allowed me to use to communicate what was happening on a daily basis. It served as our prayer journal. Through that website, we were reaching thousands of people, even internationally, all of them standing with us in prayer. The transformation of his health was an answer from God for all of us.

Justin recovered. He returned to school much wiser for having gone through such a harrowing ordeal.

The Last Second of the Game
About nine months later, Justin began finding it hard to breathe. He'd had a cold a few weeks back, but it appeared to be getting better. We took him to the bone marrow unit of the hospital. They took one look at his lungs and he was admitted immediately.

His lungs appeared to be shutting down. They could not diagnose exactly what was happening to him, but assumed it was a very late graft vs. host disease response to the cold symptoms he'd had. His immune system overreacted and began fighting against his own body.

They performed an emergency lung biopsy to see if they could determine what was causing it. That procedure was very painful for Justin to recover from.

Within twenty-four hours, he was put on life support and given every antibiotic they could think of to halt the infection. Infectious disease doctors came in and out of the room to try and determine if he had been exposed to something that might have caused it. His lungs simply deteriorated at a rapid rate and became purple, diseased, and spongy.

His body was wasting away because he was not able to take the nutrition through his nose without coughing and possibly choking it into his lungs.

We watched completely helpless.

There was more pain in my heart than I could adequately write watching him decline so quickly. I had trusted God every step on this long, treacherous journey and realized that this could be how it ended. I had allowed God access to the outcome.

I knew there was nothing I could do to halt His sovereign plan, nor did I want to. But, if He was looking for someone to take Him at His Word and believe Him to raise the dead in our culture, I would do it.

It wasn't my reputation at stake; it was His. Every part of the Bible I scanned said the Lord is pleased with our faith.

Cindy Jacobs had prophesied years before at the dedication of our new sanctuary at church that even the dead would rise in this place. I remembered thinking at the time, "Now, that would be something to see."

I had tucked it away in my heart, but I pulled it back out as I now had the choice to believe it or not. I reread the story in Luke 7: 11-17 when Jesus raised a woman's dead son. I knew in my heart that He could do it today. My question was, "Was that what He wanted to do for Justin?"

I decided to act on it, and I called my pastor, Gary Kinnaman. I told him what was happening and that should Justin die, I would like to lay his body in our sanctuary where it was prophesied that even the dead would rise in this place.

There was complete silence on the other end.

I further explained that because of legality issues I needed his help to find a mortician who would pick up the body at the hospital morgue and stop by the church before taking him to the funeral home.

Again, complete silence.

I was not crying at that moment. I was believing. The crying would pick back up after I hung up the phone. He cared about my heart. He knew this journey had lingered and we all had been through the fire. He also had to swallow the hard reality that people die, even those who stand in faith. He had archived many funerals in his years of pastoring. Horrible and painful situations that did not end in life, but rather in death.

I told him my job was to simply ask the Lord. If God chose to formally take Justin home to be with Him, that would be the decision of the Lord and I would accept that. I also knew that I didn't extend my faith for over three years in a life-and-death tug of war without showing the Lord at the end that I believed He could do whatever He wanted, even after death.

Nothing is too difficult for our God.

I did not want to regret not extending my faith past my comfort zone. I was already out this far, and going all the way out seemed exactly what the Lord was looking for.

He did what I asked and found a mortician. He put a time limit on how long Justin's body would lie in the sanctuary—thirty minutes. I told him that would be fine.

It was all set.

Then, it happened.

The lights and sirens went off in Justin's room causing every ICU doctor to run to him. His chest began to heave and I thought this was it. I slipped out into the hall and absolutely collapsed. I couldn't believe that this was how his story would end. It was completely out of my control, and all I could do was accept the reality of what was happening.

I waited in the hall for them to tell me he had passed. I saw the doctors and nurses leaving one by one, and I gathered the courage to ask if he was still alive.

Not only was he alive, but it appeared his lungs were better. I checked the website blog and an unknown visitor posted this in the prayer journal in all caps, "IN JESUS' NAME, BE HEALED."

They did an x-ray and his purple, diseased, and spongy lungs were normal.

Very slowly, they began to wean him off the ventilator. Since he hadn't eaten for weeks, his body was under eighty pounds. He had to learn to eat again, sit up again, and move his body. Little by little, this warrior came back to life.

I don't know what happened that day, but I think the Holy Spirit walked into his room and performed a miracle that only He could do. There is no other medical explanation. Perhaps the heaving in his chest was the hand of God healing his lungs.

I share all of this with you to let you know that, during this experience, God had built a faith in me that was sustainable. I came out the other side stronger for having gone through. I knew how to believe God for the miraculous. He had taught me to not look directly at my circumstances, or they would take me down.

I would attribute this experience to the grand finale of the best fireworks show you have ever seen. A shimmering, glimmering, dazzling, glowing display of the power of God. There was no other explanation for this turn of events. All anyone could do was to stand there and say, "Wow!"

Years later, City of Hope flew the donor out for a surprise visit to meet Justin and our family to celebrate their tenth anniversary of bone marrow transplants. We were shocked to learn she was from Germany. The cells had traveled internationally to reach us in Phoenix, Arizona.

Meeting her and finally being able to hug her neck and thank her meant so much to the heart of this mother. A thank you seemed inadequate for her selfless and generous donation.

She had saved my son's life.

Below is a picture of Ina Radunski, our donor. It is amazing the similarities in their genetic makeup.

Now, let's get back to how God used this faith He built in me to guide me through the gut-wrenching trauma I found myself in with my husband.

Chapter 12

It's Time to Heal

He's Still Lying

Life presents us with opportunities for growth all the time. Many times, these opportunities can come masked in pain, but if dealt with properly they can eventually bring out the best in us. I say, eventually, because shedding the cocoon of our ache and releasing the growth of our butterfly is a process that rarely happens overnight.

After my husband moved out, he continued to see the counselor on his own. He was advised to begin attending SAA (Sex Addicts Anonymous) meetings immediately, which he did.

At first, I wasn't buying that there was really a thing called sex addiction. It appeared to me to be a label used to continue a pleasurable activity. It took a while, but I would learn to understand that it was real and it was his drug of choice to compensate for the pain he was in.

I, on the other hand, walked around like Old Faithful, ready to erupt at any moment. This geyser erupts around twenty times a day and can last ten minutes in duration.

I walked into my bank to make a deposit one day and as I stood at the teller window, she pleasantly asked me, "How are you doing today?"

I opened up my mouth to give the pat answer, "Fine," but there was nothing about me that was fine. As I opened my mouth to answer her, my lips trembled and I began to weep uncontrollably. It was embarrassing, and that poor young girl felt helpless to console me.

Grief waits for no one.

Kindness goes a long way, and being sensitive and ready to extend compassion to a fellow man, even if they are a complete stranger, was something I learned from this journey.

All my life, God had healed every emotional pain I had. He had earned the title of being my Wonderful Counselor, and I trusted Him with everything. But this pain of betrayal was excruciating and I needed help quickly before it suffocated me.

I went to the grandfather of all search engines, Google, to explore what options were out there. I stumbled across SAA meetings that were available for spouses of sex addicts.

My body walked into that first meeting intact, but my heart was so shattered I didn't even recognize myself.

The meeting began with the twelve steps being recited, just like at a regular AA meeting. We were then instructed to stand to our feet, state our name, label our identity with a disease, then sit down. It was all geared toward taking responsibility for ourselves.

I watched as a room full of thirty beautiful women, all different ages, robotically stood to their feet and recited what they were told to do.

I couldn't do it.

I wasn't going to own a label identifying a behavior I had not done. The only label I owned was the label that I was a child of God and adopted into His family. That was my identity.

I strongly believe in owning one's behavior, but in this setting, I felt like I was being instructed to own my husband's behavior.

This was what I walked away with that night:

- I was told that I had to be a codependent.
- I was told that there was something intrinsically wrong with me because I had married a sex addict.

I found both of these labels to be less than helpful in bringing me comfort. It actually inflicted more pain than anything.

I drove home that night and had a long talk with God. I said, "If my husband decided to rob a bank after thirty years of marriage, is there something wrong with me because I married a bank robber?"

No, there was nothing wrong with me. I had nothing to do with the choices my husband made. My husband was a good man, a good husband, and he provided well for his family. We had a strong and healthy sexual relationship, but along the way, he made the destructive choice to dabble in porn and slipped into an addiction that pulled him into a depravity in his mind. He violated his own body, the bodies of other women, and my body.

The mindset that the spouse is equally responsible for these decisions is ridiculous. I hurt for all the other women there and vowed that I would find something else to comfort women at this stage of recovery.

I was referred to a female pastor to look at areas of codependency in me. We were reading through a book and I came to realize that I had over-functioned in my marriage. I did entirely too much in raising the children, running the household, and working the business.

My over-functioning gave my husband all the free time he wanted to create this secret life. I repented for that and asked the Lord to change that inside of me.

This pastor began to counsel me that I needed to forgive my husband and reconcile. To be honest, that is exactly what I wanted. But something did not resonate inside of me.

Everyone in my life had their opinion of what my next steps should be. It was exhausting because my mind felt like a ping-pong ball going back and forth over the net of staying or leaving.

In the initial months of our separation, my husband and I decided to both run our company as we had done for thirty years. It was a great income. I needed a job, and it seemed fair. He would stop by the house with orders and pick up things he needed regularly.

During these times, he shared what he was learning at his SAA meetings. He seemed sincere. However, I was covertly watching his behavior for signs of lying as he spoke. He had mastered the art of deception. He had manipulated me for ten years. Now that his secret was out in the open, would he really want to turn his heart back home to be the husband and father God had called him to be?

I read books about watching body language to determine when someone was lying. The slightest movement of these master manipulators is all it took. I hated the fact that I didn't see any of this when it was happening right in front of me.

I learned that when he made a slight crossing of his ankles or a crossing of the arms while speaking, he was covering up a lie. All the while, he was completely able to look me straight in the eye.

To show that he was sincere and willing to change, he brought over his old computer which he had broken into pieces. He said he had turned off the highway, gotten out of the car, and smashed it. He hated what he had become. He bought a new computer and asked me to put a program on it so that he would be accountable to avoid the porn websites.

When he stopped by four days later, I was not at home. He asked my son if I had installed the safety program on his new computer, and he said that as far as he knew, I hadn't. I hadn't told anyone that I had taken it to a friend who installed a good tracking program for me. I carefully packaged it back up as if the computer had never been opened and left the box right where he had put it by the front door.

This would become my front-row seat to watch from afar the mind of a serial liar. This new lie detector computer would display the truth I needed.

He was very convincing with his verbal updates that he was healing and getting the help he needed. He was telling me what I wanted to hear. But the Lord had chosen to actually show me the truth with my own eyes and that truth would set me free.

One particular Sunday, he stopped by the house after his church service. I knew before he got there that he had been up all night long, building his cyberspace, sexual perversion world. He had used his webcam to Skype for sexual favors with more women than I thought possible.

He walked in happy. He read me the notes he had taken on the pastor's sermon. As he spoke, I observed every movement like a newly-hired CIA agent.

I listened as he spoke to me in a high-pitched giddy voice. He said God was speaking to him and he was changing. But I knew the truth, and it wasn't what he was saying. The truth was he hadn't slept all night and the perversion in his mind had taken center stage in his heart.

The only indication that he was lying was he crossed his ankles. That's it! That is what I had missed for ten years.

I learned he had a secret phone. My son decided to check his car the next time he came over. He found it in the middle console and took it.

We read, with sadness, the multiple texts he had sent to numerous women just minutes prior. He was pledging marriage to them, none of them knowing about the others.

I fought the urge to phone them all and tell them the truth. My place was to swallow the whole truth and let that truth set me free. When he realized his phone was missing, he came back and got it.

He had been found out. Again.

His game of charades had been exposed, and I was not going to be tricked a second time. The man he continued to pretend to be was no resemblance to the man he was when I married him.

My question now was, could God heal this?

I believed, with all my heart that He most certainly could.

Wrestling with God

Even with all the new proof of him continuing with his deceit and betrayal, I desperately wanted God to reconcile and heal our marriage because I believe that the covenant of marriage is holy to the Lord.

One morning in prayer, I heard the Lord say, "Silence the voices." I was drowning in a sea of others' opinions. Some well-meaning friends were adamant that I should divorce, while others were equally adamant that I should reconcile. The only opinion that mattered to me was what the Lord said for me to do.

My marriage was His gift to me, and I knew He would lead me if I could just quiet my heart and the voices of others and listen to Him.

My pastor was placed as the shepherd over my heart, and he was truthful and deeply honest with me as to the reality and depravity of what I was dealing with. He reminded me that this behavior did not surface overnight. It had taken ten years to get his mind entrenched into this behavior and the hope of reconciliation seemed impossible.

I wanted nothing more than for God to show His best work with this impossible situation. I wanted Him to heal my husband. I wanted Him to restore our family. I had witnessed His power in healing my son. My faith was ready to believe Him once again.

Can dead things rise? Yes, they can!

I came up with a plan that I would seek God every morning from 5:00 am to 7:00 am for a week. I silenced all the other voices as the Lord instructed me to. I would wait on God in prayer in the stillness of the early morning to show me what my next steps should be.

I was exhausted. I was emotionally drained. I still cried uncontrollably in the night. My mind was tormented with the destruction of my life as I had known it. It seemed easier to just curl up in a ball somewhere. But a decision had to be made, and I wanted clarity from God's heart to make the one that would be His best.

The first morning, I rolled out of bed at 5:00 am and laid prostrate on the floor. I sobbed deep ugly cries for the first thirty minutes. I couldn't have prayed if I wanted to.

There were no words.

Those sobs pierced the early morning and made me feel like I was hyperventilating. I was holding in the volcano that wanted to spew out to avoid upsetting my children who were within earshot.

The Lord knew I was trying to call out to Him with everything I had. I just had nothing to give Him. My body was showing up, but my emotions were as raw as I'd ever known them to be.

The Lord was tender with me. My sobs became my prayer. They were the only thing my body was capable of at that time.

Gently, I heard the Lord speak to me. "You are at a crossroad, and you have two options. The path of divorce or the path of reconciliation. The choice is yours."

I answered, "Lord, the path of divorce is not an option. I made a commitment to YOU when I married, and I will keep that commitment and not dishonor you."

In my mind's eye, I began to journey toward the path of reconciliation. I sensed confusion, frustration, and no peace. The Lord would gently say, "May I show you the other path?"

"No, Lord! You hate divorce. I will not dishonor You," I replied.

This went on for days. The same exact scenario repeating itself. Each morning, the Lord asked me which path I would choose, and I chose the path of reconciliation. The path of divorce was not an option. There was no peace in my heart for six days as I tried with everything inside of me to reconcile my marriage before the Lord.

Gently, the Lord began to address my resistance. He said, "Yes, I hate divorce, but I also hate lying and deceit. I have given you a way out. I am releasing you from the commitment due to the sin of adultery."

I was wrestling with God because I had a stronghold in my mind that was deeply embedded. It was a false belief system that believed under no circumstance would divorce ever be an option for my life. I had signed my marriage certificate with my own blood, so to speak. If I had not allowed the Lord access to my faulty thinking, the trajectory of my days ahead would have had a completely different outcome.

On day seven, the Lord asked me the same question and this time, with some fear and trepidation, I said, "I will try the path of divorce."

As I took those initial steps forward in my mind, all of that dissipated and each step was filled with peace. It began to build stronger and stronger with each step. I began to feel a freedom I had not felt before. It was undeniable and overwhelming as the peace of God was confirming what my next steps should be.

There was no mistaking that the Lord was guiding me with His peace.

How could something I was so adamantly against be my ticket to freedom?

I learned something so valuable from this experience about the peace of God. It leads us. When a decision needs to be made and life presents a fork in the road, get alone with God and seek His peace for your solution.

The Ram Will Be There
Perhaps I am guilty of overthinking, but my faith doesn't let go just because life gets hard. The Lord has trained me to believe in the impossible. I had convinced myself that this answer of divorce was simply a test of my obedience.

In Genesis 22:2, God asked Abraham to take his son Isaac and go up the mountain and sacrifice him. Isaac was the promised, long-awaited son, the apple of Abraham's eye. Despite what his emotions felt in the moment, Abraham moved in obedience to the Lord's request. Up the mountain he went, holding the hand of his son, but at the last minute, God provided a ram in the thicket to be the sacrifice instead.

Isaac and Abraham lived happily ever after.

My marriage was my Isaac. In obedience, I, too, was walking up my mountain, overriding my emotions, and holding the hand of my marriage to sacrifice to God. I wanted my storyline to read something like this:

Barbie trusted God. She went up the mountain to sacrifice her beloved marriage in obedience to God. Then, at the last minute, God stepped in and stopped the divorce. He healed everyone and restored the marriage.

I held onto this hope of restoration as each day proceeded into the next.

The day of filing came. It was February 2nd, 2015. My husband and I met at the courthouse in Mesa, Arizona. We were amicable. There were no attorneys. I had baked him a plate of his favorite brownies and cookies. I attached a note for him to read later. In it, I thanked him for the past thirty years.

I wished him the very best in his healing journey. I told him that I believed that he was not the type of man who would degrade women like this. I reminded him of the man he was when we first met. By all outward appearances, he was a man after God's heart. It ended with a prayer for God's healing upon his life.

I'll be honest with you; that was the *second* letter I wrote.

The first one I wrote had a judgmental overtone to it. It screamed of the hurt and pain that was torturing my heart and our children for his selfish actions. But I knew how important words were, so I tore it up and started again. The Bible says in Proverbs 18:21 that our words hold the power of life and death in them.

I thought about the fact that these words could possibly be the last ones I would ever speak to him. I wanted those words to be a blessing, not a curse. I definitely had to override my emotions to rewrite a positive, life-giving message.

The papers were filed by him.

Something happened that day at the courthouse that I will never forget. The atmosphere was electric and filled with a grandiose sense of angels celebrating. It was like they were having a party and were excited. It was all the more reason for me to believe that maybe God was still going to stop the divorce.

The Lord whispered in my ear to remember the date, February 2nd, "2/2", and to remember the address of the courthouse, 222. Later, I would learn the significance of 2's. They were a reward. The Lord said to me, "Not only am I going to give you back double for your trouble, but I am also going to reward you three times over for all that was taken from you."

From that day on, I saw the numbers "22," and "222" everywhere. I would wake up in the middle of the night at exactly 2:22 am, night after night. I would smile and knew it was the Lord reminding me of his promise. I saw it on license plates, addresses, websites. Each time those numbers appeared, it was a reminder to hold onto his promise of reward.

It was a comfort to me in the long lonely days that lay ahead. Even the verse about Abraham in Genesis 22:2 had the numbers in it.

God had provided a ram in the thicket for Abraham, but He did not provide a substitute ram for me, as I had hoped. I walked up that mountain by faith—a faith that required steps of pain. With each step, I continually remained hopeful and aware that the answer was just beyond what I could understand.

I believed until the last moment for God to turn it around, but God knew things I didn't. My marriage ended on that mountain and I came back down that mountain single and having to face life alone, broken, and deeply shattered.

Moving Forward
Months had marched on and I was still stuck in my pain. I was shredded inside with rips to my heart that I had no idea how to mend. Little by little, I followed three paths to find relief.

1. Online support groups
2. Personal Growth Seminars
3. Date with Shannon

I joined an online support group for women who were dealing with the consequences of their husbands' sexual indiscretions. In this group, I learned I was not as alone as I felt. I may have been dumped into adulterous waters, but one thing was for sure, I had no desire to stay there treading these murky waters for the rest of my life.

I learned that there were other women out there trying to recover and swim to shore to find some new stable ground to rebuild on.

After a few months, I became aware that many were using the forum to vent and rip venomously at the mere mention of their spouse's name. I understood.

The pain of this type of betrayal was never intended for the delicacy of the feminine heart. The desire to make their husbands pay was enormous, and they had a strong desire to take vengeance into their own hands.

I was fighting against bitterness, too, and I felt that if I allowed myself to continue reading their words, I would never advance past where I was. My pain was still so deep. I knew enough of God's Word to know that if I used my words to seek revenge of any kind it would lead to *my* downfall, not his.

Without my constant awareness of that reality, I could have easily plunged into allowing my anger to take root and turn to bitterness. Each time my heart turned in that direction, the love of God would meet me there and remind me of His Word. It was always with tears and heartache that I would stop and turn around in my heart. It seemed unfair and unjustified to turn away from it, but because I loved God and I trusted Him, I did it as an act of obedience.

I was invited to attend a personal development seminar called PSI Seminar. It was a way to challenge myself to explore and question the ways I "show up" in life and question the ways I don't "show up."

To be honest, I felt too old to try and reinvent myself at this season of my life. That, of course, was not true, but it was how I felt. On Saturday night, we played a game. There were one-hundred of us, altogether. They broke us up into two teams. I cannot recall exactly how the game was played, but I will always remember what I learned from the outcome of that game.

Sometimes, "the only way to win is to stop playing the game."

See, the only way for a team to win was for everyone on that team to be in agreement with a decision that was made. The game was full of calculated moves much like moving a chess piece. As the decisions came one after another, you started to develop strong convictions of not agreeing with the majority, but to disagree meant the entire team could not move on.

We either had to all be in agreement or all be in disagreement. It was most difficult for that brave soul to stand alone in their conviction and to take the heat and frustration from the rest of the team.

When my head hit the pillow that night, I remember thinking that in many ways I was playing a game I didn't even know I was playing. By continuing to play, I was allowing myself to be used as a pawn.

The only way for me to win was to stop playing, fold, and walk away.

When there are only two players in a game and one player stops playing, the game ends. Period. That revelation, spoken in that way, made me feel like the winner in my situation with my husband for the first time.

I shed many tears that weekend, but I walked away with an awareness that I was painstakingly moving forward, albeit inch by inch. I was learning to shake off the debris left in the wake of utter destruction produced by one man. That was another revelation—he was only one man.

I was not going to define myself by one man's choices. I took ownership of myself and for the future choices that I would make. I took ownership to heal.

Pray for Him

Six months into my healing, I felt stuck. I didn't feel like I was progressing. The pain was still assaulting my heart relentlessly. I was struggling to move past the residue of the destruction. That is, until my dinner date with Shannon. Shannon was a worship leader at a neighboring church. We were sent to dinner on the dime of a friend who knew us both. He felt our stories were similar and I approached this dinner thinking that, because I was the older of the two of us, I would be helping her.

That was not how it worked out.

We met at a restaurant. She was young, beautiful, and kind-hearted. I knew right away that the love of God flowed generously from her heart. We began to share our stories. Back and forth we went, each of us able to empathize with the other. Her story was full of betrayal and adultery and a ripping and tearing of her heart. I hated that she had to walk that road at such a young, tender age.

A simple question from her would be the catalyst that would catapult me past being stuck.

"Do you pray for your ex?" she asked.

Emphatically, I answered, "No!" I had purposely decided months before to untie any apron string or soul tie of attachment I had to him. I was concerned that if I continued to pray for him, I would continue to care.

She began to explain how God instructed her to pray for her ex-husband. She described the verse in the Bible in Matthew 5:44 that God commands us to love our enemies and bless those who hurt you and say all manner of evil against you.

I sat there in silence. I knew that verse, and I knew she was right. Withdrawing was a decision that I had made out of my pain. The only way through the pain all the way to the other side was to be obedient to this verse and to do what the Lord commanded, even if my flesh didn't feel it.

Where in the word of God does it say to not pray for someone who hurt you for fear of remaining attached to them?

It doesn't.

She went on to tell me how the Lord had given her a strategy to accomplish this. "Trust me," she said. "In the beginning, I didn't want to do it, either."

These are the prayers she shared with me that the Lord told her to pray:

- Bless the work of his hands
- Bless him from the top of his head to the bottom of his feet
- Bless his relationship with the new woman

She laughed and said, "God told me to pray those things like I mean it, and not with an attitude."

I left that evening with an instruction from the Lord in my heart to return to praying for my ex-husband.

I was motivated because I wanted my pain to end. She told me, "Pray every time you feel the pain, even if that means every minute."

That would be through the night and every minute of the day because, without exaggeration, that was the constant prick on my heart.

Day one came and went and it felt like I prayed non-stop. It didn't seem to make a difference. The pain in my heart lingered.

Day two appeared to be the same. I prayed all through the day and through the night.

- I prayed that God would heal him.
- I prayed for his job to be successful.
- I even prayed that God would bless the relationship with the woman in his life, and I did it with sincerity.

On day three, I stepped outside to do my daily walk. I had been pounding the pavement, walking and praying for months. It was my therapy. I think my neighbors may have thought I was crazy because I sang and prayed out loud as I walked down the street night after night.

I was looking forward to walking and listening to a new song I would be singing at church on Sunday titled, "What a Beautiful Name it is," when I heard the gentle whisper of the Lord ask me, "How are you doing?"

I thought, "Good, Lord."

Then He asked again, "No, how are you doing?"

It hit me like a ton of bricks. At that moment I realized that I had not experienced the jabbing pain in my heart for at least the past three hours. That constant, torturous, ongoing, relentless pain I had been wrestling with every minute of every day had stopped. I looked up into the night sky and said, "Thank you, Lord."

This part of my healing came because I did exactly what God said to do. I prayed for the man who deeply hurt me as if my own life depended on it. It seemed counterintuitive to do that when pain was coursing through my veins, but it's actually brilliant.

Praying for those who've hurt you has a boomerang effect. The more you pray for your enemies, the more the blessing of those words return to heal you!

What a strategy!

Praying for those who have hurt you disables a root of bitterness from attaching itself to your heart. When we give ourselves over to the pain, the blame, or the victim role, it's like inviting bitterness to come and be your constant companion.

Think about that! If you are struggling with someone who dumped on you and poorly treated you, they are only one person.

Let them go! Hide yourself in prayer and pray for them openly and honestly until the weight of their offense is removed from your mind.

Some people lose a spouse in death, others through divorce. There are those who divorce that will stay connected for the sake of raising the children. That was not my story.

Mine was a complete break. Unfortunately, my ex-husband did not stay in contact with either one of his children. When he left, he left as if those thirty years of our life had never happened.

There was no funeral, no eulogies, and no closure. When God stepped in that morning and gave me those eight words that would change my life, He did it to rescue me, not to torture me. I had to trust Him for the way out which nearly seemed impossible.

I don't know what your story is, but I know that God specializes in the impossible, and if you would dare to take His Hand and entrust your brokenness to Him, He will lead you out, too.

For me, I learned that the quickest way through my pain was to allow Him to do the breaking and to stop resisting what the pain was trying to accomplish deep inside of me.

God's fingerprints are evident in my story and in my whole life. He has made something beautiful out of every hopeless mess I found myself in.

He can do that with you. Give yourself over to the One who created you. He knows what to do. He has so much more for you than you could ever think, ask, or imagine.

Chapter 13
Guided by Dreams

The Powerful Subconscious

Surprisingly, the average person spends about twenty-six years sleeping during their life, which equates to 9,490 days, or 227,760 hours. Did you know that your subconscious mind is powerful and completely alert while you are sleeping?

At night, your subconscious mind is free from the interference of daily life and has nearly all the resources of your brain at its disposal. It stores your beliefs, your previous experiences, your memories, and your skills.

Everything that you have ever seen, done, or thought is stored in your subconscious mind.

God uses different means to personally speak to us. He may speak through another person, an image, a phrase, a feeling, and even through dreams. When a dream repeats on multiple nights, pay attention. Ask the Lord if He is speaking to you.

There are many nights while you are sleeping the Lord will give you dreams many of which are preparatory or directional for your future.

Throughout the Bible, God spoke to many in their dreams and gave them direction.

   a. Abimelech (Gen. 20:3-7)

   b. Jacob (Gen. 28:12; 31:10)

c. Laban (Gen. 31:24)

d. Joseph (Gen. 37:5-9)

e. Pharaoh's butler and baker (Gen. 40:5-19)

f. Pharaoh (Gen. 41:1-7)

g. Midianite (Judges 7:13-15)

h. Solomon (1 Kings 3:5-15)

i. Nebuchadnezzar (Dan. 2:1, 31; 4:5-8)

j. Daniel (Dan. 7:1-28)

k. Joseph (Matt. 1:20, 21; 2:13-20)

l. Wise men (Matt. 2:11-12)

m. Pilate's wife (Matt. 27:19)

God still speaks to us in dreams.

I want to encourage you to journal your dreams and pay attention to their messages.

A great dream interpretation book I use is *The Divinity Code to Understanding Your Dreams and Visions,* by Adam F. Thompson and Adrian Beale.

I had two preparatory dreams before the revelation of my husband's behavior. There was a bus dream and an ocean rescue dream. At the time they didn't make sense, but later they would bring enormous comfort.

Bus Dream
This bus dream was a recurring dream that happened months before and I couldn't understand its meaning. In this dream, I was in the home of a young woman I barely knew in Kansas. Her husband had gone to college with my son and I met them both just a few times. I was in her kitchen. She was pregnant and facing me as I was speaking to her when suddenly a bus crashed through the right side of her kitchen wall. My father was driving it. Before I could yell, "Dad!" the bus turned into a

train and crashed through the left side of her kitchen wall leaving absolute destruction.

I could understand that the dream was an analogy of what had happened with my father. What I didn't know was that it would soon be repeated with my husband. What entered into my life as one thing would exit as something completely different.

God will often speak to us in our dreams using symbols, much like how he spoke in parables while He was on the earth. It is in our best interest to put in the effort to decipher the meaning.

Rescued from the Ocean Dream
The second dream happened seven days before the Lord tapped me on the shoulder and gave me the message to check my husband's computer.

In this dream, I was being rescued from the ocean by two Navy SEALs. I knew that I had been out in this ocean for quite some time, alone and treading water to stay alive. It was in the middle of the night. There was no light. I was surrounded by darkness. I saw a child of about four years old near me. Her head had just dipped into the water as if she was drowning when all of a sudden, a very bright light shone from above. A helicopter had come to rescue me.

The child that I had seen was no longer there as the two Navy SEALs came down with a rescue stretcher. They strapped me in and sent it back up to the helicopter.

Once inside, my body began to go into severe shock. They removed my wet clothes and wrapped me in a thermal blanket. I was still in shock and one of them said, politely, "I am going to lay my body on you to get your body temperature stabilized."

The other one said, "I am going to put these headphones on your ears to block out the noise."

I remember that, in this dream, I felt absolutely exhausted, but safe.

They took me to a hospital, and after several hours, came to check on me. I thanked them for rescuing me and keeping me warm with the blanket and body heat and for the headphones.

They looked confused and said, "Ma'am with all due respect, we didn't do any of those things. You were strapped to the stretcher in the front of the helicopter and we were strapped into our seats in the back because we were traveling through a war zone."

Then I woke up.

This dream became clear all on its own seven days later.

In my initial days of shock, the first dream was understood to be the same enormous identity change that happened to my father happened again, but this time to my husband. What was once a bus, within seconds became a train. The devastation left behind in the kitchen (which usually describes the heart) was my reality. Though it was two different kinds of sexual perversion, the message rang clear that the men I knew one minute would not be the same in the next.

Once my initial shock began to thaw, I remembered the second dream. I realized that the Lord had seen me alone in that ocean of deceit, a place where no one else knew I was, not even myself. I believe the child was my inner child slowly dying. The Lord had sent two of His finest 'Navy SEAL' angels to rescue me.

I did a study on US Navy SEAL training and their qualifications are unparalleled to any training a human being can survive.

The comfort I received was from the Lord, Himself, as the Navy SEALs said they did not do those things. I was hospitalized, traumatized by the event, and in need of healing. This was my story, foretold to me in a dream.

Lost Purse Dream
There was another dream I had a few months before the ocean rescue. In this one, I was in some kind of dorm lying on the top bunk of a bunk bed when, suddenly, I realized that I had lost my purse.

I leaped off the top in a panic to go find it. Suddenly, there was a fireman who got up from the bottom bunk and said, "I'll help you." He was dressed in a navy blue t-shirt, yellow fireman's pants, and yellow suspenders.

I wondered how long he had been there. I hadn't known that anyone slept on the bottom bunk. Together, we went and retraced my steps at a library I had been to. I was disappointed each time I thought I would find it, only to realize it wasn't there.

It seemed like a very long time, but my purse was finally found at the library. Along the way, the fireman and I had gotten to know one another. Once the pressure was off and my purse was found, I was able to relax as we walked back to the dorm.

I enjoyed talking to him. He asked me if I would like to join him for lunch. We had been looking for the purse for so long, I didn't realize how hungry I was. I sat across the table from him and I could sense that he was attracted to me.

He had kind eyes, a sincere smile, and a gentleness about him.

Then I woke up.

I asked a friend to interpret it for me and she said anytime we are trying to find a lost purse it symbolizes finding our identity. In the course of finding that rediscovery, I also found a possible love interest. I tucked the dream away.

Offensive Coach Dream
I was hired by three NFL coaches to be the offensive coach of an already existing team. I know nothing about the game of football, so I decided to let the players call their own plays.

After seeing my strategy, the three coaches that hired me called a special meeting and made it clear that I had to call the plays and the team could only do what I said.

I began to make up plays.

No matter what I told this team to do, we won.

We won game after game after game until every radio show and news station wanted to interview me.

They all asked the same question, "Coach, what's your strategy?"

I would look directly into the camera and say with utmost sincerity, "I don't know what I'm doing."

No one believed me. They credited me with being the humblest of all coaches. My team respected every play I called without question.

But the truth is, the plays were ridiculous. In one game, we were tied right up to the end and the quarterback asked me, "Coach, what's the play?"

I told him, "Get out on that field and count down. Make sure you have eleven players on the team." That was the play.

Imagine the quarterback running out into this stressful moment and calling the team to count down to eleven. Are we all accounted for? Break, this is it.

I am laughing just thinking about the stupidity. But the team thought it was brilliant.

I was the Elle Woods (from *Legally Blonde*) coach of the offense. I walked along the sidelines carefree in my heels and my matching outfits, oblivious to the game, and yet, no matter what I said, respect, success, and fame came my way.

I woke up from that dream in the middle of the night drenched in tears because I had been laughing so hard. I fell out of bed and continued laughing hysterically on the floor for a good fifteen minutes until my sides were splitting.

The three coaches in this dream represented the Father, the Son, and the Holy Spirit. They have hired me for a task, and I truly believe that this dream was preparing me to write this book.

In the darkest of days, I hung onto these dreams as personal words to me from the Lord. He had spelled out the journey of discovery, healing, and a new beginning before any of it hit my life, simply by putting me to sleep. This gave me great comfort on the very difficult and lonely days that I have had to walk.

God can start your life over again with a new beginning at any season and at any age.

I have learned that feelings change as grief swells and falls, so they must take second place under my faith. Today, I live my life with the awareness that God supplies all I need in His timing. He is a God of abundance and those who belong to Him lack no good thing.

Faith is living with the eager anticipation of good things happening every single day!

Barbie Durham

Chapter 14

The Solution

The effects of my father's perversion would drip upon my life with disdain, shame, remorse, and pain for most of my life. I didn't do it, but nonetheless, I was forced to deal with the fallout.

Whether you know it or not, the sexual perversion rampant in our culture today has perversion dripping over all of us.

Regardless of what society deems acceptable, the sexual issues we are dealing with have a spiritual component attached to them. To ignore that spiritual component is taking our nation down deeper and deeper into our own depravity.

I'm borrowing the famous line from the 1995 movie *Apollo 13* to ask us all to reconsider these issues by looking through the lens of God.

"Houston, we have a problem!"

Five-year-old children are now given the option by their parents—persuaded by a society that thinks that if a child believes they should be the opposite sex, then they should—to start hormone therapy, and this is well before puberty.

Pornography is beyond out of control and ripping apart individuals and marriages. We've succumbed to sex trafficking our children because the slippery slope God warned us about in the Book of Proverbs was ignored. Homosexuality is on the rise.

I have asked God why He doesn't destroy us like He did Sodom and Gomorrah. Certainly, we are worse now than they were.

But He is a God of mercy, and He extends His love toward us to give us time to repent and to heal our land.

So, where do we start?

We start by returning to the originator of our sexuality. God has something to say, but it will require a ripping of our own flesh and a repentance to return to the original design.

That's what revival looks like.

We are going to have to swallow the hard truths of what 1 John 2:16 warns us are the biggest obstacles in our world regarding perversion. We all struggle with them to one degree or another.

- The lust of the flesh
- The lust of the eyes
- The pride of life

God is not a killjoy, and neither am I. I believe we can all agree upon this one truth:

Sex is absolutely, unmistakably the best gift God ever invented.

All He asks is that we enjoy it within the boundaries He created.

He understands that the temptations against this boundary are flitting about on our computers, movie screens, and magazines bombarding our minds daily and pulling as many as will follow them down the path of perversion.

He created us male and female to be united as one flesh in the holy bonds of matrimony. We were created to live monogamous lives without adultery or fornication, giving our bodies fully to our spouse of the opposite sex.

God spoke to me in prayer one day and asked me this question: 'If Hugh Hefner can build a mansion of perversion, would you build Me a mansion of purity?'

It seems a daunting task to go against the tide of our culture and I don't at all feel qualified for the job, but if God wants me to do it, then my answer to Him is resoundingly, "Yes, Lord."

I am motivated because I believe in marriage. I believe the institution is purposely used by God in His Word to reflect His purity and His heart of love for humanity. He longs to come back for His bride to find her spotless, without wrinkle or blemish.

If I can make a difference in your life, and you make a difference in someone else's life, together we can build Him this mansion of purity.

My prayer is that it will stand out like a lighthouse as an alternative for many to steer clear of this storm of perversion crashing in the darkness.

The starfish story, adapted from an essay by Loren Eiseley, is a perfect example of the effect one person can have in turning back this tide.

An old man walking along the beach at sunrise came upon a young man sifting through the debris left by the night's tide. Every now and then, he picks up a starfish and flings it back into the sea.

The old man asked him the purpose of his efforts. "The tide has washed the starfish onto the beach. They will die unless I throw them back," the young man replied.

The old man looked around at the miles of beach. "There are more starfish than you could ever save. Surely you cannot expect to make a difference."

The young man bent to pick up another starfish. As he sent the starfish sailing back to the water, he said to the old man, "I can make a difference to this one."

Will you help me build a mansion of purity for God?

Acknowledgments

To my friend, Ricki Trejo, for having the guts to walk up to me at the tender age of twelve to tell me that God loved me. Your courage changed the whole trajectory of my life.

To my pastor, Ron Hart, for being like Jesus and becoming a father to the fatherless by finding homes in the congregation for my siblings and me. Your love and care covered our orphaned hearts with the love of Jesus.

To my foster parents, Neil and Kitchie Julien. Thank you for taking me into your home and providing for me during a very difficult and painful season in my life. Your generosity kept me out of the state foster care system and taught me what a healthy home environment looks and feels like.

To my college friend, Joanne Saunders, for telling me about your charismatic church during our years together in college. Your invitation changed my life and introduced me to walking in the gifts of the Spirit.

To my friend, Vicki Ingle, for being a godly mentor since I was in my early twenties. Your investment in me has shaped me to be the woman I am today. Thank you for believing in me and for praying for me to receive the gift of speaking in tongues.

To my pastor, Dr. Gary D. Kinnaman, thank you for investing in me for thirty years and allowing me the space to develop my spiritual gifts under your leadership. Your communication style, candor, and use of humor while speaking to an audience was something I wanted to emulate, as well as your unique ability to bring God's Word to life. Thank you for walking with our family as our pastor all those years through premarital counseling, officiating our wedding, dedicating both of our children, and praying for all of us through Justin's illness.

To my friend, Beverly McIntyre, you called out the prophetic gift in me and taught me how to develop it, how to wear the armor of God, and take my stand in the authority of God. You've loved me since I was twenty-two years old and believed the best in me.

To our NFL football player, Damon Dunn. Thank you for your generous investment into our family and your obedience to God to come to the hospital for that season and pour into each of us. Your love for God and your fortitude taught us to stay in our fight, and that every battle is won in the last three seconds of the game, no matter who is in the lead.

To Justin's bone marrow donor, Ina Radnuski, thank you for giving him the lifesaving donation of your cells. Your selfless generosity saved his life and we will be forever grateful to you.

To Cindy Jacobs, your prophetic gift was used by God powerfully in my life and in the life of my son. Thank you for being generous with your gift and for stepping out in faith. You showed up and God did the rest.

To Shannon Lutz, for your godly advice to follow God's pattern to pray for my husband, even after the pain he caused me, and to bless him so that the final deliverance of my own pain would be released. You were spot on with that advice. Thank you for that dinner date.

To my publisher, Eli Gonzalez, you were sent to me by God. I held this book inside of me for nine years and God used you to get it out. Your amazing gift to write and to write in such a way as to reach the reader's heart was in the back of my mind as I put pen to paper. Your faith in God and your own personal story touched me deeply, and I felt safe to expose the 50-year secret of my father for the first time under your leadership.

About the Author

Barbie Durham was born in Oceanside, NY. She graduated from Grand Canyon University with a major in counseling and a minor in biblical studies. She is a speaker to women's groups, and has served her church in intercession for pastors. She is a Toastmaster and earned second place in the state of Arizona for an inspirational speech contest. She is a certified health coach, helping many find health in mind, body, soul, and spirit. She is passionate about teaching others how to walk the Christian life guided by the Holy Spirit. She teaches from the Word and from experience, and has gained credentials—as she puts it—from the School of Hard Knocks. She is the mother of two adult children, Justin and Carissa, and currently resides in Tempe, AZ.

Barbie loves to stay active. She loves to travel. If you would like to invite Barbie to your event, she can be reached at barbie22sing222@gmail.com or her website www.barbieinreallife.com

Made in the USA
Monee, IL
14 June 2021